When FOOTBALL *Was* FOOTBALL

NOTTINGHAM FOREST

First published in 2013

A catalogue record for this book is available from the British Library

ISBN: 978-0-85733-203-5

Published by Haynes Publishing, Sparkford, Yeovil,
Somerset BA22 7JJ, UK
Tel: 01963 442030 Fax: 01963 440001
Int. tel: +44 1963 442030 Int. fax: +44 1963 440001
E-mail: sales@haynes.co.uk
Website: www.haynes.co.uk

Haynes North America Inc., 861 Lawrence Drive,
Newbury Park, California 91320, USA

Images © Mirrorpix

Creative Director: Kevin Gardner
Designed for Haynes by BrainWave

Printed and bound in the US

When
FOOTBALL *Was*
FOOTBALL

NOTTINGHAM FOREST

A Nostalgic Look at a Century of the Club

Ivan Ponting

Contents

Introduction

To a whole generation of football fans, a mention of Nottingham Forest conjures up an image of one arresting individual – Brian Clough. But although the self-styled "Ol' Big 'Ead" looms as an undeniable colossus in the history of this venerable institution, as even the most casual thumb through these pages will verify, the City Ground has thrown up a whole host of colourful characters and unforgettable football men over the last century or so.

Having entered the Football League in its fifth season, 1892–93, Forest quickly became stable members and lifted their first major silverware, the FA Cup, towards the end of Queen Victoria's reign.

There followed a lengthy period of yo-yoing between the old Divisions One and Two, with the next major landmark being another FA Cup triumph in 1959 under the enlightened management of Billy Walker.

The 1960s brought sustained status with Johnny Carey's lovely team featuring the starry likes of Joe Baker, Ian Storey-Moore and Bobby McKinlay once finishing as championship runners-up to Manchester United, but the early 1970s brought relegation – and then came Clough.

Such was the scope of Forest's transformation that they regained the top flight in 1977, lifted the League title a year later and then followed up with the little matter of winning the European Cup in both 1979 and 1980.

The heroes of that rarified time – John Robertson, Viv Anderson, Martin O'Neill, Peter Shilton et al – march across these pages in all their glory as the Clough years stretch to 1993, which brought retirement for the turbulent boss and demotion for his team.

Since then there have been varying fortunes, but here the whole riveting story is brought to life through the magnificent *Daily Mirror* pictorial archive, from which countless gems have been unearthed.

When Football Was Football – Nottingham Forest offers a feast of nostalgia, evoking people and places and occasions which will never be forgotten by those who love the Reds, or those who simply can't resist the romantic lure of a departed age.

Seeds of the Forest
1865-1939

A gentle training jog for feisty full-back Percy Barratt (left), Irish international centre-half Gerry Morgan (centre) and centre-forward Randolph Galloway (right) as Forest prepared to fight for their Second Division lives in the spring of 1926.

1865 Forest are founded at a pub, the Clinton Arms, long since demolished. 1866 First official game, against Notts County, with Forest fielding 17 men to their opponents' 13. Result reported variously as 0-0 and 1-0 to Forest. Rules bore little relation to modern game. 1878 Reds enter FA Cup for first time, beating Notts County 3-1. 1879 Club leaves the Forest Racecourse to take up residence at The Meadows. 1880 Forest move on again, this time to Trent Bridge. 1882 Still footloose, the club relocates to Parkside, in the Lenton part of the city. 1885 Remaining in Lenton, Forest now shift to the Gregory Ground. 1889 Club joins the Football Alliance, the level below the Football League. 1890 Forest's sixth home is the Town Ground. 1892 Reds enter the Football League. 1898 Forest win the FA Cup and move into the City Ground, where they put down roots at last. 1906 Relegated from top flight. 1907 Forest are Second Division champions. 1911 Demoted again. 1922 Forest win the Second Division title again. 1925 Another relegation.

Forest Up and Running

A group of enthusiastic young players of a game known as "shinney" – in all likelihood a corruption of "shinty", a particularly vigorous early form of hockey – decided to have a go at an increasingly popular pastime that was gaining ground in Sheffield, and which had recently spawned the formation of Notts County.

They took to football – for such was their new passion – with such eagerness and enjoyment that the inevitable outcome was the formation of a club, which quickly developed as a rival to the pioneering Magpies.

In the early years they wandered from location to location before settling at the City Ground and growing into a major power in the land. They weren't always successful; after joining the Football League there were periodic downs as well as ups, but it was clear by the early part of the 20th century that Nottingham Forest was an institution that would endure.

England goalkeeper Sam Hardy was close to his 38th birthday when he was recruited by Nottingham Forest in August 1921, but he proved to be an inspired signing for the Reds, starring as the Second Division championship was lifted in the following spring.

Hardy, who had made his name with Liverpool and Aston Villa, was one of the most famous footballers in the land and proved that his ability had not withered with age as he conceded only 23 goals in 32 games during Forest's triumphant campaign. He remained at the City Ground until 1924 when injury forced the veteran finally to lay aside his gloves at the grand old age of 41.

When
You're
Smiling...

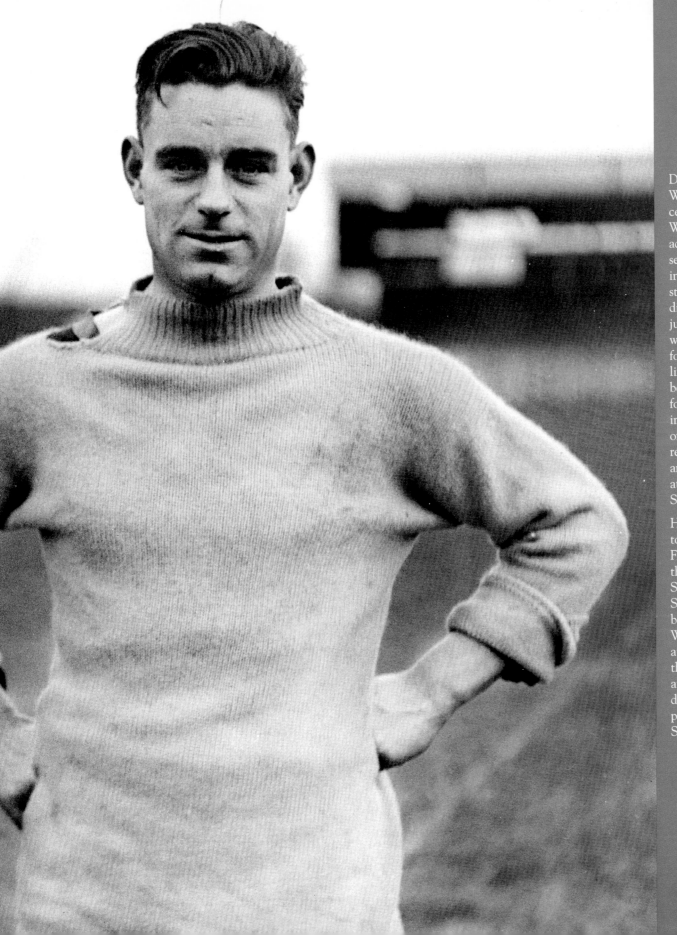

Dynamic wing-half Bob Wallace (left) and reserve centre-forward Duncan Walker smile through adversity during a training session at the City Ground in February 1926, with the striker looking to be in dire need of a replacement jumper. The campaign was proving a grim one for Forest, who had found life among the elite to be unremittingly difficult following their promotion in 1921–22. Three years of struggle culminated in relegation in 1924–25, and now they were toiling at the wrong end of the Second Division table.

However, consolation was to be found in a courageous FA Cup run during which they beat Bradford City, Swindon Town and Southend United, only bowing out to Bolton Wanderers after two replays at the quarter-final stage. In the League they narrowly avoided a second successive demotion, finishing four points clear of relegated Stoke City.

Forest skipper Bill Thompson (right) and his Sheffield United opposite number Billy Gillespie do the honours before kick-off in their FA Cup quarter-final clash at Bramall Lane in March 1928. The Blades triumphed 3-0, leaving the Reds to finish their Second Division season in mid-table mediocrity.

Full-back Thompson was one of the club's bulwarks during a troubled era, making nearly 400 senior appearances between 1922 and 1935, serving a stint as a popular captain in the wake of Bob Wallace.

The jovial referee here is the charismatic Captain Albert Prince-Cox, a former impressionist on stage who went on to become the king's weather consultant and manager of Bristol Rovers, although not at the same time.

The Walker Way
1939-1960

Heroes to a man. Inspirational skipper Jack Burkitt perches precariously on the shoulders of Tommy Wilson (left) and Jeff Whitefoot as he shows the FA Cup to Forest's ecstatic supporters after beating Luton Town at Wembley in 1959. Stewart Imlach, voted Man of the Match, waves the lid of the famous old trophy, while next to him Johnny Quigley grins contentedly. On the right of the group Billy Gray has custody of the plinth, while popular trainer Tommy Graham beams at the cameras.

1939 Billy Walker takes over as manager. 1947 Reds consolidate mid-table position in Second Division. 1949 Forest reach lowest ebb, slipping into Third Division (South). 1950 Club narrowly misses bouncing back up at first attempt. 1951 Promoted as champions. 1952 Walker's team only two points shy of reaching First Division. 1957 Runners-up to Leicester City, promoted to top flight; run to quarter-finals of FA Cup. 1959 Forest win the FA Cup for the second time.

New Boss Fires Forest Ambition

Having stood the test of nearly three-quarters of a century by the outbreak of the Second World War, Forest had become a familiar part of the national football scene, even though they had scarcely rivalled the stellar likes of Arsenal and Aston Villa, Liverpool and Everton, even Huddersfield Town and Blackburn Rovers, in the business of winning trophies.

New boss Billy Walker was made of stern stuff, though, and he resolved to change all that. Still, for some years it was a question of two steps forward and one step back before he guided Forest to a place among the elite in 1952, then strove to scale the game's loftiest summits. He made it to one of them, with a rousing FA Cup triumph at decade's end, but that elusive League crown would have to wait for another messiah …

Full-back Geoff Thomas was one of the most loyal of all Nottingham Forest servants, making 429 League and FA Cup appearances for the club between his debut in 1946 and his farewell in 1960, when he lent a valuable hand as the Reds narrowly escaped relegation to the Second Division.

Having been a first-team regular throughout the late 1940s and most of the 1950s, the faithful Thomas was unlucky to lose the number three shirt to newcomer Joe McDonald in 1958–59, thus missing out on FA Cup final glory in the twilight of his career. However, he collected a medal for his integral role in winning the Third Division (South) championship in 1951 and remained influential as Forest rose from the Second Division in 1957.

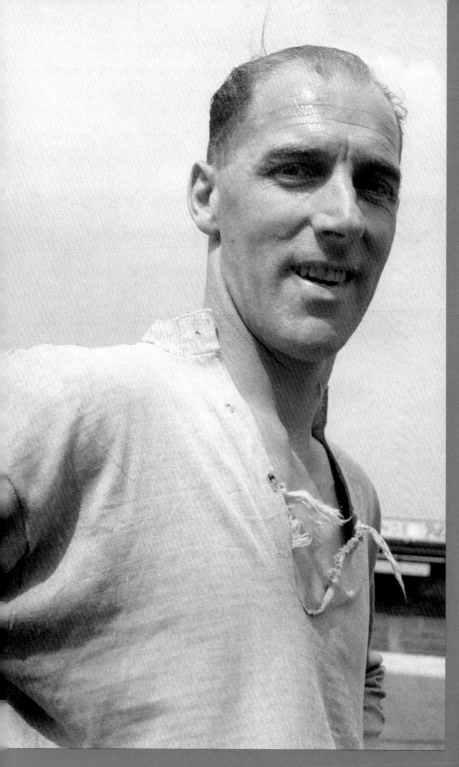

BELOW: Jack Hutchinson was the thinking man's full-back, a canny operator skilled at jockeying opponents away from the danger area and a shrewd reader of the ever-changing action. He was brave, too, a brisk tackler at need, and made more than 250 senior appearances for Forest in his 13 seasons at the City Ground, a tenure which began immediately after the Second World War. Hutchinson's total would have been far more extensive, but for the presence of Geoff Thomas and Bill Whare, who were also eminently reliable flank defenders during the 1940s and 1950s.

ABOVE: Harry Walker was a consistently excellent goalkeeper during the decade after the Second World War. Having served Darlington and Portsmouth before the conflict, he was signed by Forest as a 30-year-old in April 1947, and was still performing capably when injury forced his retirement eight years later.

Wally Ardron, Forest's record-breaking sharpshooter.

Wally Ardron

After punchless Forest had slipped dismally into the Third Division (South) in 1948–49, manager Billy Walker sought a proven goal-getter to revive their fortunes, and he found just the man in Wally Ardron. The rugged, pacy Yorkshireman, a former railway fireman, had not long shattered Rotherham United's seasonal scoring record, and although he was not far short of his 31st birthday – having lost his early prime to the Second World War – Walker judged the £10,000 fee to be a sound investment.

Duly Ardron obliged, hitting the net 25 times in his first campaign at the City Ground, then plundered 36 – still a Forest record – as Walker's men lifted their divisional title in 1951. Ardron was a dasher, a study in perpetual motion as he sprinted to all attacking areas, an irresistible force in the air and carrying an explosive shot in either foot. He was remarkably courageous, too, nothing loath to fling himself among the flailing boots and an intimidating proposition for any would-be marker. There wasn't much delicacy to his game, but nobody at the City Ground was worried about that as the goals flew in.

Ardron retired in 1955, having struck five hat-tricks for Forest and become a local folk hero. He died in 1978.

FOOTBALL –STATS–

Wally Ardron

Name: Walter Ardron

Born: 1918

Died: 1978

Playing Career: 1938–55

Clubs: Rotherham United, Nottingham Forest

Forest Appearances: 191

Goals: 124

A Born Entertainer

A Forest forward line train with the camera in mind at the City Ground ahead of the 1950–51 campaign which would end with the Third Division (South) title safely gathered in. Right-winger Freddie Scott (far left) and left-winger Colin Collindridge (far right) were both ever-presents in the victorious campaign. Inside-forward John Love (second left) made only a handful of appearances, while spearhead Wally Ardron (centre) hit the target 36 times, missing only one match.

But to many fans, the key man was inside-forward Tommy Capel (second right), who contributed 23 goals and created as many scoring opportunities as he converted. The tall Lancastrian was a born entertainer, especially adept with his left foot, which he developed into such a potent weapon only after a boyhood accident to his right. He was a persuasive dummy salesman, too, capable of wrong-footing an entire defence with a single shimmy.

BELOW: For nearly a decade and a half after the Second World War, Bill Morley was one of the most versatile footballers at the City Ground. At his best as an industrious wing-half – he didn't miss a game as Forest achieved promotion from the second tier in 1956–57 – he also played in all five forward positions, and had made more than 300 League and FA Cup appearances for the club before losing his place to the younger Jeff Whitefoot in 1958–59.

ABOVE: Horace Gager was an archetypically tough and unyielding centre-half who might have won plenty of England caps but for losing his playing prime to the Second World War. As it was he joined Forest from Luton Town in February 1948, and was ever-present as they collected the Third Division (South) crown in 1951, the same year in which he was appointed captain in succession to Bob McCall. Off the pitch he could cut an aloof figure, but there was no denying the force and value of his contribution to the Forest cause before he retired, aged 38, in 1955.

The Recipe for Success

Forest keeper Harry Walker is poised to save as a Reading forward heads for goal at the City Ground in January 1951, while defender Geoff Thomas can only look on, helpless to intervene. The game finished 1-1, with Roland "Tot" Leverton netting for the hosts, who were destined to be crowned champions of Third Division (South) at season's end.

The team constructed by manager Billy Walker – no relation to the net-minder – finished the campaign in dominant form, winning seven of their last eight games to leave them six points clear of runners-up Norwich City.

Walker achieved his success thanks in no small measure to fielding a settled side, comprising a core of only 12 players, nine of whom totalled more than 40 appearances. The mighty dozen were goalkeeper Walker, full-backs Bill Whare and Thomas, centre-half Horace Gager, wing-halves Bill Morley and Jack Burkitt, wingers Freddie Scott and Colin Collindridge, free-scoring centre-forward Wally Ardron, and inside-forwards Tommy "Tucker" Johnson, the much-loved Tommy Capel and Leverton.

Meadow Lane is bulging with a close-to-capacity crowd of 44,000 as Forest custodian Harry Walker plunges bravely at the feet of County's England international marksman Frank Broome in the Trentside derby of September 1951. Defender Geoff Thomas is on hand to mop up if necessary.

The game finished 2-2, with strikes by the visiting Colin Collindridge and John Love cancelling out efforts by Broome and Bobby Crookes on a day when County's star performer, the great Tommy Lawton, failed to hit the target.

Of the two clubs, newly promoted Forest were far more satisfied with their season, finishing a creditable fourth in the Second Division table, while County languished in the bottom half, only five points clear of the drop.

ABOVE: The healing hands of Forest masseur Bob Davies prepares right-back Bill Whare for action ahead of the Trentside derby at Meadow Lane in October 1956, which the Reds won 2-1 on their way to promotion glory in the spring.

Guernsey-born Whare was a City Ground stalwart throughout the 1950s, his grip on the number two berth so tenacious that the faithful Geoff Thomas was switched to the left flank.

RIGHT: Two players have eyes only for the camera, while one keeps his gaze firmly on the ball during a training session at the City Ground in autumn 1956. Left to right are forward Peter Higham, goalkeeper Harry Nicholson and full-back Geoff Thomas.

Higham peaked during the previous campaign, when he netted 16 times in 39 games, while Nicholson enjoyed two mid-1950s campaigns as Forest's first-choice net-minder. As for Thomas, he was rarely absent from the action throughout the entire decade.

Keeper Chic Thomson plucks the ball from the air to prevent a corner against Portsmouth during Forest's 4-1 victory at Fratton Park in September 1957. Thomson, who collected a League championship medal with Chelsea in 1954–55, had recently arrived from Stamford Bridge, manager Billy Walker having decided that the Scot would prove invaluable in helping the Reds to consolidate their place in the top flight. Thomson did just that, bringing extra confidence to the rearguard as Forest finished a commendable 10th in the First Division table.

Eddie's Back in Triumph

It was as if he'd never been away! Garrulous Londoner Eddie Baily (second right), one of Tottenham Hotspur's wonderful push-and-run side of the early 1950s, returns to White Hart Lane as Nottingham Forest captain for a League encounter in October 1957. Here he talks over old times with his opponents for the day, left to right, Terry Medwin, Mel Hopkins and Spurs boss Bill Nicholson, a team-mate of Baily's as the north Londoners became Second and First Division champions in successive seasons.

At the end of a thrilling afternoon, it was Eddie Baily (centre) who was happiest, as his side had triumphed by the odd goal in seven. Here he chats to vanquished opponents Bobby Smith (second left) and Terry Medwin, one of Spurs' scorers. That's Forest custodian Chic Thomson on the left and full-back Geoff Thomas on the right.

On the Road to Wembley

Johnny Quigley lurks in readiness for a loose ball as Tooting and Mitcham goalkeeper Roy Seckers and two of his defenders combine to deal with a Nottingham Forest cross in the FA Cup third-round clash at the Isthmian League club's Sandy Lane headquarters in January 1959.

The Reds' knockout charge, which was destined to end in Wembley glory, almost stalled at the starting line as Tooting led 2-0 with only a little more than half an hour left to play. However, Billy Walker's men escaped with a 2-2 draw, courtesy of an own goal and a Billy Gray penalty, and won the City Ground replay 3-0 with Roy Dwight, Tommy Wilson and Stewart Imlach all registering.

Forest number eight Johnny Quigley looks on as Grimsby keeper Alan Barnett flies through the air to repel a long-range effort in the FA Cup fourth-round encounter at the City Ground in January 1959. The hosts cruised to a 4-1 victory courtesy of two strikes by Billy Gray, including a spot-kick, and one each from Jeff Whitefoot and Tommy Wilson.

Beating the Blues

A heading duel between Forest centre-forward Tommy Wilson and Birmingham City's England international full-back Jeff Hall proves inconclusive, as did this FA Cup fifth-round clash at St Andrews in February 1959. The game finished 1-1, with Wilson supplying the visitors' goal.

Tragically, the talented Hall was to die of polio only a few weeks later.

ABOVE: With Forest central defensive bulwark Bobby McKinlay standing guard, keeper Chic Thomson makes a smart save in the FA Cup fifth-round second replay against Birmingham City at Filbert Street, Leicester. The first replay, in Nottingham, was a 1-1 draw, with Roy Dwight netting for the hosts. This time, though, it was one-way traffic, with Billy Walker's team hammering the Blues 5-0.

BELOW: Neither for the first nor the last time in Forest's 1959 FA Cup run, right-winger Roy Dwight finds the net. This was part of the chunky marksman's hat-trick in the 5-0 fifth-round drubbing of Birmingham City in the second replay at Filbert Street. Billy Gray contributed the other two goals, one of them a penalty.

Triumph over the Trotters

Tommy Wilson knocks home his own and Forest's second goal on the way to dumping holders Bolton Wanderers out of the FA Cup in a pulsating quarter-final at the City Ground on the last day of February 1959. The Trotters' England goalkeeper Eddie Hopkinson can only gaze impotently as the ball speeds past him into the net. The hosts won 2-1.

ABOVE: Forest's Scottish international left-winger Stewart Imlach looks exhausted as he is mobbed by jubilant supporters after the tense FA Cup quarter-final triumph over Bolton. Had it not been for the police protection, his progress to the dressing room might have taken considerably longer.

Forest's Famous Five

The club's forward line in all nine FA Cup matches during the victorious 1959 campaign trains together at the City Ground after disposing of holders Bolton Wanderers in the quarter-final. Jumping for joy are, left to right, Roy Dwight, Johnny Quigley, Tommy Wilson, Billy Gray and Stewart Imlach.

Forest manager Billy Walker insisted on a high level of ball skills, even from his full-backs, as demonstrated here by Joe McDonald (left) and Bill Whare, training at the City Ground in March 1959 during the run-up to the FA Cup semi-final against Aston Villa.

Semi-final Success

ABOVE LEFT: As Forest fans pack the Hillsborough terraces ahead of their FA Cup semi-final against Aston Villa in March 1959, the banner on the right says it all. Those who paid to watch the team week in and week out loved them to play "The Walker Way", which was generally attractive and exhilarating with the accent on attack. This game had added significance for the Forest boss in that he had spent his glorious playing career with Villa, while his first managerial achievements had been for Sheffield Wednesday, who were hosts for the day.

ABOVE RIGHT: When crowd control was a gentle affair: "Forester", one of the club's chief cheerleaders, chats to the local constabulary before the semi-final.

Forest centre-forward Tommy Wilson is thwarted by a combination of Aston Villa centre-half Jimmy Dugdale and goalkeeper Nigel Sims during the FA Cup semi-final. Wilson, a pacy former winger, was a tough opponent for any defender to pin down, but the man who made the difference in this tense Midlands battle was inside-right Johnny Quigley, who scored the only goal of the game.

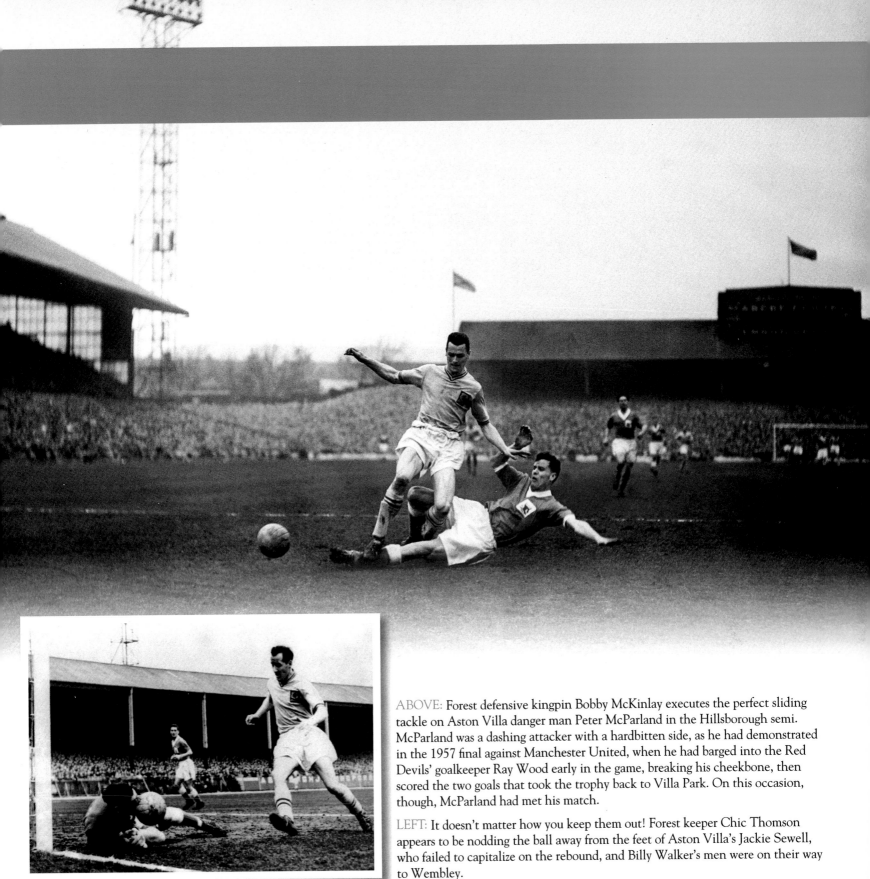

ABOVE: Forest defensive kingpin Bobby McKinlay executes the perfect sliding tackle on Aston Villa danger man Peter McParland in the Hillsborough semi. McParland was a dashing attacker with a hardbitten side, as he had demonstrated in the 1957 final against Manchester United, when he had barged into the Red Devils' goalkeeper Ray Wood early in the game, breaking his cheekbone, then scored the two goals that took the trophy back to Villa Park. On this occasion, though, McParland had met his match.

LEFT: It doesn't matter how you keep them out! Forest keeper Chic Thomson appears to be nodding the ball away from the feet of Aston Villa's Jackie Sewell, who failed to capitalize on the rebound, and Billy Walker's men were on their way to Wembley.

35

FOOTBALL
–STATS–

Billy Walker

Name: William Henry Walker

Born: 1897

Died: 1964

Playing Career: 1915–33

Clubs: Aston Villa

England Appearances: 18

Goals: 9

Managerial Career: Sheffield Wednesday, Nottingham Forest

LEFT: Billy Walker and Forest became synonymous during his long and distinguished reign as City Ground boss.

BELOW: One of the perks of being Forest boss Billy Walker's wife was having his football medals made into a bracelet.

–LEGENDS–

Billy Walker

Billy Walker was the enlightened manager who guided Nottingham Forest into the postwar age, creating a team that was both entertaining and successful, and his crowning achievement was lifting the FA Cup in 1959.

By the time of his arrival at the City Ground in March 1939, the football-obsessed Midlander had already forged a shining reputation in the game. As a player he had been a free-scoring marksman with Aston Villa and had captained England, and as a boss he had led Sheffield Wednesday to FA Cup glory in 1935.

However, his Hillsborough sojourn ended in acrimony after the Owls were relegated and he resigned in late 1937, then putting in a brief stint with non-League Chelmsford City before accepting the Forest reins.

Walker's first job was to avert demotion to the third tier that spring, which he achieved before global conflict reduced sport to an irrelevance. After the war he was lumbered with a club in disarray and a poor squad, but managed to avoid relegation until 1949, when they finally made the drop.

A dynamic, resilient character and a student of the continental game, Walker now set about transforming Forest's fortunes, launching a much-needed youth policy and bringing in experienced players to create a decent side, which won the Third Division (South) championship in 1951.

Thereafter he continued to rebuild cannily while espousing an open, exhilarating brand of football which yielded promotion to the top tier in 1957. Then came FA Cup euphoria two years later. In 1960, suffering from declining health, Walker retired, having created a sturdy platform for the club's future development. He died in 1964.

Forest Fever

It was some time before kick-off, as can be deduced from the gaps on the Wembley terraces, but these two ardent Forest fans were already cheering on Billy Walker's men, who were due to face Luton Town in the FA Cup final later that afternoon.

Ready for the Fray

LEFT: Forest skipper Jack Burkitt manages to raise a smile, but the mounting tension is written all over the faces of everyone else in the Wembley tunnel before the showdown with Luton. The Hatters' captain Syd Owen awaits the call to action with folded arms, while his team-mates are equally solemn. Behind Burkitt, goalkeeper Chic Thomson and full-back Bill Whare look impatient to get going, while their boss Billy Walker (right) cannot disguise the strain.

BELOW: Forest centre-forward Tommy Wilson exchanges pre-match pleasantries with the Duke of Edinburgh, while Bobby McKinlay and Joe McDonald (right) await their turn for the royal handshake.

Forest Dominate the Hatters

Forest took the lead only nine minutes into the game when Roy Dwight (out of picture to the left) surged on to a delightful pull-back from left-winger Stewart Imlach to crack the ball high into the Luton net. It was the climax of a lovely flowing move which summed up Forest's early dominance. Play-maker Jeff Whitefoot dispatched a characteristically elegant delivery from the centre circle towards the left touchline, Billy Gray nodded it on to the flying Imlach, who gulled his marker Brendan McNally before sending in Dwight to apply the finishing touch.

This time Luton's England international goalkeeper Ron Baynham thwarts the rampant Roy Dwight, whose afternoon is soon to be disrupted agonizingly.

Forest spearhead Tommy Wilson soars into a gap in the Luton rearguard to net Forest's second goal with a powerful header from a diagonal Billy Gray cross. Only 14 minutes had passed and the Reds appeared to be in total control, but the easy flow of the game was about to be transformed.

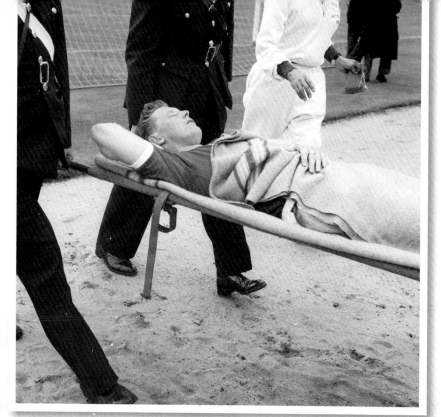

Agony for Goal Hero

LEFT: Goal-scorer Roy Dwight is stretchered from the pitch after his leg was broken in a 33rd-minute accidental collision with Luton full-back Brendan McNally. In those dark days before the use of substitutes, that meant that Forest had to soldier on for an hour with only 10 men, but although their attacking impetus was inevitably jolted, they didn't forsake their customary neat, polished style.

BELOW: Luton keeper Ron Baynham scoops the ball away from Forest predator Tommy Wilson, who was attempting to add to his earlier goal. The Hatters' captain, Syd Owen, looks on calmly.

ABOVE: Just after the hour mark, Luton reduced the arrears to 2-1 when their number six, wing-half Dave Pacey, smacked a shot past Chic Thomson from eight yards. That set up a last half-hour that was thrilling for the neutral, but nerve-jangling for the Forest faithful.

BELOW: Luton's likeliest saviour as they chased the game in the last 30 minutes was former Scottish international Allan Brown, who went close to grabbing an equalizer on several occasions. Here he is foiled by Forest keeper Chic Thomson, who has left his line to block the Hatters' marksman with his feet.

They Shall Not Pass!

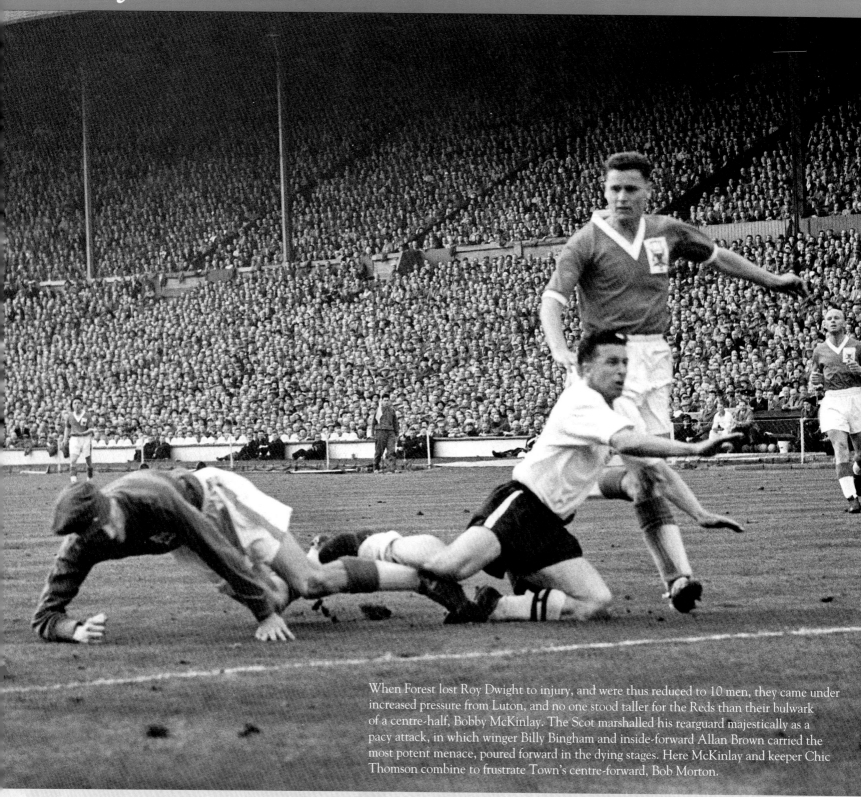

When Forest lost Roy Dwight to injury, and were thus reduced to 10 men, they came under increased pressure from Luton, and no one stood taller for the Reds than their bulwark of a centre-half, Bobby McKinlay. The Scot marshalled his rearguard majestically as a pacy attack, in which winger Billy Bingham and inside-forward Allan Brown carried the most potent menace, poured forward in the dying stages. Here McKinlay and keeper Chic Thomson combine to frustrate Town's centre-forward, Bob Morton.

All energy spent, rival skippers Syd Owen of Luton and Forest's Jack Burkitt stroll off together at the end of 90 minutes' enthralling action, with the sporting Owen congratulating Burkitt on the victory. There was personal consolation for Owen in what had otherwise been a traumatic season, with the Hatters being relegated to the Second Division, in his selection as Footballer of the Year, the decision being announced the day before the final.

Jack Burkitt's finest hour: the Forest wing-half and captain performed superbly in the 1959 FA Cup final triumph over Luton, toiling mightily for an hour after his side had been reduced to 10 men, and he richly deserved his celebrations at the end of an unforgettable afternoon.

FOOTBALL
–STATS–

Jack Burkitt

Name: John Orgill Burkitt

Born: 1926

Died: 2003

Playing Career: 1947–62

Clubs: Nottingham Forest

Forest Appearances: 503

Goals: 15

Managerial Career: Notts County

In the middle years of the 20th century, professional footballers tended to be expert at snooker, too, many of them heading for their local billiards hall straight after training to while away those long afternoons. Here Forest skipper Jack Burkitt lines up a shot to the middle pocket, watched closely by centre-forward Tommy Wilson.

–LEGENDS–

Jack Burkitt

Jack Burkitt was one of the finest footballers in the land never to win an England cap. A stylish wing-half, he read the game perceptively, he was pacier than his long-striding, seemingly ponderous gait suggested, and he was powerful in the air, as befitted a former centre-half. The tall Midlander passed the ball safely and sensibly too, and he was a crisp tackler.

True, he faced a bevy of formidable rivals for essentially defensive midfield berths in Walter Winterbottom's side. During Burkitt's 1950s heyday he was up against the likes of captain Billy Wright, the incomparable young leviathan Duncan Edwards, the ultra-consistent Jimmy Dickinson and the dapper Ronnie Clayton, so maybe a regular slot was beyond him, but it seemed perverse that he wasn't offered a single opportunity.

For his only professional club, however, Burkitt excelled for 13 seasons following his debut in 1948–49, lining up in a classy half-back line alongside Horace Gager and Bill Morley, and he emerged as a natural leader, becoming in 1959 the only Forest man in the 20th century to lift the FA Cup.

That afternoon at Wembley, when the Reds were reduced to 10 men following the injury to Roy Dwight, Burkitt's energy and intelligence were major factors in that landmark triumph for the club.

Jack in the (Royal) Box

A moment to savour, and to remember all the days of his life. Forest captain Jack Burkitt, having climbed the famous 39 steps to the royal box at Wembley, holds high the FA Cup.

ABOVE: Didn't we have a loverly time the day we went to … Brighton and Hove! Centre-forward Tommy Wilson (left), goalkeeper Chic Thomson and their respective wives stroll along the prom on the Sunday as Forest treat the players and their families to a day at the seaside to celebrate the second FA Cup triumph in their history.

RIGHT: Roy Dwight leaves Wembley hospital on crutches on the Monday after the FA Cup final in which he notched the opening goal. His life would never be quite the same again. Before suffering a broken leg against Luton, Elton John's cousin – that would become Dwight's other claim to fame – had been a fabulously prolific marksman, netting

57 times in 80 senior games for his previous club, Fulham, then adding 29 in 50 outings for Forest following his £6,000 transfer from Craven Cottage to the City Ground in the summer of 1958.

He was equally effective on the wing, where Billy Walker employed him for the Reds, or at centre-forward, where he had often lined up for Fulham. Sadly, he was never the same potent force following his injury, and he finished his League career with brief stints at Coventry City

and Millwall. Dwight died in 2002, but he will be remembered forever by the grateful fans of Nottingham Forest.

Coming Home with the Cup

Nottingham Forest's coach emerges from the city's railway station with skipper Jack Burkitt proudly brandishing what was, at the time, the most precious piece of silverware in the domestic game. Ahead was a tour of Nottingham with fans lining the route, roaring and cheering as they waited patiently for a glimpse of the coveted old pot.

–LEGENDS–

Stewart Imlach

Scottish international winger Stewart Imlach was a dashing tearaway raider who played the game with verve. He spent only the second half of the 1950s at the City Ground, but during that incident-packed tenure he established himself firmly as a favourite of the fans, contributing hugely to promotion from the second tier in 1957 and FA Cup final victory over Luton Town two years later.

Indeed, he was voted Man of the Match at Wembley, setting up the first goal for Roy Dwight and playing a part in the build-up to the second, supplied by Tommy Wilson.

Unlike his unfortunate countryman Bobby McKinlay, Imlach won Scottish caps, four of them, including two at the 1958 World Cup finals in Sweden.

The diminutive dark-haired Scot entered the English game with Bury in 1952, then followed a brief stint with Derby County before his switch to Forest in the summer of 1955. At the City Ground he blossomed entertainingly, specializing in cutting inside to shoot at the goal with either foot, but he was also adept at reaching the byline, usually the prelude to a telling cross.

Most Forest supporters were dismayed by Imlach's departure to Luton in June 1960. He was still in his prime at 28, had starred in the club's greatest day of the century and yet was judged surplus to requirements.

ABOVE: Forest's left-wing dasher Stewart Imlach receives the *Daily Herald* trophy as Man of the Match in the FA Cup final against Luton Town. It was a richly deserved prize, the Scottish international having played a part in creating both goals in the 2-1 victory, then ran himself to a standstill as the 10 men of Forest had to step up their workrate following the first-half injury to Roy Dwight.

A born opportunist, Stewart Imlach escapes the attentions of Tottenham's John Ryden (left) and Mel Hopkins to lift the ball over advancing keeper Ron Reynolds during Forest's 4-3 win at White Hart Lane in October 1957.

FOOTBALL
–STATS–

Stewart Imlach

Name: James John Stewart Imlach

Born: 1932

Died: 2004

Playing Career: 1952–67

Clubs: Bury, Derby County, Nottingham Forest, Luton Town, Coventry City, Crystal Palace

Forest Appearances: 204

Goals: 48

Scotland Appearances: 4

Goals: 0

Bobby McKinlay, putting in the hard yards ahead of the successful 1956–57 campaign.

Bobby McKinlay

Name: Robert McKinlay

Born: 1932

Died: 2002

Playing Career: 1949–70

Clubs: Nottingham Forest

Forest Appearances: 685

Goals: 10

The sun beats down on Bobby McKinlay at the City Ground in August 1963.

–LEGENDS–

Bobby McKinlay

Bobby McKinlay looms over Forest's postwar history like the colossus he was. The tall, composed, commanding Scot was the trusty defensive rock on which successive sides were built in the 1950s and 1960s. He was a reassuring presence during the reigns of Billy Walker, Andy Beattie, Johnny Carey and Matt Gillies, and why he was never called to his country's colours, despite frequent recommendations by club bosses and Scotland scouts, remains one of the game's more perplexing mysteries.

The consistency of McKinlay's performance and his fitness levels were remarkable. After a rare injury forced him to miss Leeds United's visit to the City Ground in April 1959, he didn't miss another game until October 1965, an astonishing sequence of 265 consecutive appearances.

The nephew of between-the-wars Forest stalwart Billy McKinlay, Bobby was recruited from Scottish amateurs Bowhill Rovers in 1949, replaced Horace Gager as regular centre-half in 1954 and went on to compile a club record of 685 senior outings. He gave a majestic display in the 1959 FA Cup final triumph over Luton Town and was the natural long-term successor to Jack Burkitt as captain, leading the team from 1962 to 1966, when Terry Hennessey took over.

Jeff Whitefoot (left) keeps his eye on the ball in training along with fellow half-backs Bobby McKinlay (centre) and Jack Burkitt.

Jeff Whitefoot

Name: Jeffrey Whitefoot

Born: 1933

Playing Career: 1951–68

Clubs: Manchester United, Grimsby Town, Nottingham Forest

Forest Appearances: 285

Goals: 7

-LEGENDS-

Jeff Whitefoot

Jeff Whitefoot was a thoroughbred performer, a creative wing-half who could pass the ball with uncanny accuracy and control it assuredly with either foot. He was a shrewd anticipator of the unfolding action, too, which enabled him to break up countless attacks with unexpected interceptions and then launch sudden counter-raids which resulted in plenty of goals.

Unflappable, always seeming to have time to play the ball, and beautifully balanced, Whitefoot impressed Matt Busby sufficiently to make him Manchester United's youngest ever player at 16 years and 105 days when he made his senior debut in 1950, and at that point in his development it seemed inevitable that he would graduate to fully fledged stardom as a Red Devil. But then a young fellow named Eddie Colman appeared on the scene, Duncan Edwards laid incontestable claim to the other wing-half berth and England under-23 international Whitefoot moved on to Grimsby Town of the Second Division.

Forest boss Billy Walker had always admired him, though, and recruited him to the City Ground cause in July 1958. He was an immediate success, helping to win the FA Cup in 1959, meshing beautifully with inside-forwards Johnny Quigley and Billy Gray, and was still excelling under former United team-mate Johnny Carey in the mid-1960s. Whitefoot retired in 1968, and went on to become the charming landlord of a succession of pubs.

Close to Glory with Gentleman John
1960-1975

Tumble drier? What's that? This was the scene at the City Ground in January 1960, when a propped washing line was very much a necessity. The young lad with the ball at his feet might be the laundry lady's son, who by the look of his uniform is just out of school and has popped in to his mum's workplace on his way home.

1960 Andy Beattie replaces Billy Walker as manager. 1963 Improving Forest reach last eight of FA Cup; Johnny Carey takes the reins. 1965 Carey leads Reds to fifth place in top tier. 1966 Unexpected demotion dogfight, drop escaped only narrowly. 1967 Runners-up to Manchester United in title race, beaten by Spurs in FA Cup semi-final. 1968 Main stand at City Ground destroyed by fire; Ian Storey-Moore scores in six successive League games. 1969 Matt Gillies replaces Carey as manager; Forest flirt with demotion again. 1972 Relegated to Second Division; Dave Mackay is the new manager. 1973 Yet another new boss, Allan Brown, takes charge. 1974 Forest reach quarter-finals of FA Cup, losing to Newcastle only after three games.

Carey's Captivating Creation

After the trail-blazing exploits of the unforgettable Billy Walker, Forest needed another visionary, and eventually they found him in Johnny Carey. The man who had reached the top of the game as a player with Manchester United, then garnered managerial experience with Blackburn Rovers, Everton and Leyton Orient, was at the peak of his powers when he picked up the Forest gauntlet in 1963.

Duly he created a lovely team, one that invariably served up entertaining fare even in adversity, and in 1966–67 they reached a glorious peak, tilting at the League and FA Cup double. Sadly for all who march beneath the banner of the Garibaldi Reds, they narrowly missed both targets, but Carey's creation – assembled so expertly and without the wealth of the big-city battalions – will always live in the memory of those fans lucky enough to have watched them on a regular basis.

Geoff Vowden, 18 years old and on the verge of turning professional, trains at the City Ground in January 1960. The Yorkshire-born, Jersey-raised marksman soon graduated to the first team and he did well, netting 45 times in around 100 games. However, his opportunities were restricted following the signing of Frank Wignall, and in November 1964 he was sold to Birmingham City for £25,000. After spending seven seasons with the Blues, Vowden moved on to Aston Villa, where he finished his League career.

A New Beginning

This was the squad awaiting new Nottingham Forest manager Andy Beattie when he replaced the long-serving Billy Walker in September 1960. Back row, left to right: Jack Burkitt, Tony Barton, Bobby McKinlay, Chic Thomson, Roy Patrick, Johnny Gill. Middle row: Roy Dwight, Johnny Quigley, Billy Gray, Tommy Wilson, Colin Booth, Billy Younger. Front row: Joe McDonald, Jeff Whitefoot, Jim Iley, Geoff Vowden.

ABOVE: Jimmy Greaves (left), arguably the most lethal British marksman of the 20th century, is frustrated by Forest's young keeper Peter Grummitt at Stamford Bridge in April 1961. It was Greaves' last game for Chelsea before moving to AC Milan and he wasn't too bothered by this momentary frustration because he scored all the Pensioners' goals in a 4-3 victory. Looking on are Chelsea's Bobby Tambling and Jim Iley of Forest.

RIGHT: Not the most elegant of postures for Forest keeper Peter Grummitt, who is in the act of dropping the ball at Goodison Park, which allowed Everton's number nine, Alex Young, to pounce for the Toffees' first goal in a 2-0 victory. It's a tad harsh to highlight this incident, because Grummitt was one of the finest net-minders in the land throughout the 1960s – but it's a terrific picture! Also in shot are Forest defenders Joe Wilson, leaping at the far post, and Bobby McKinlay.

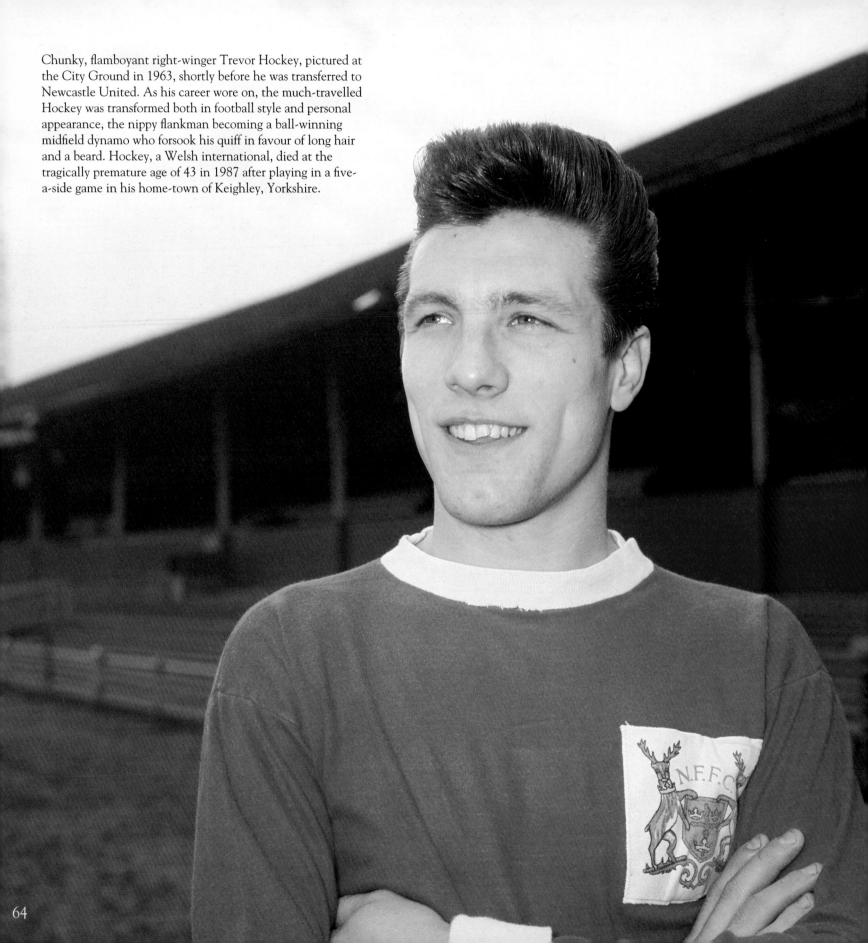

Chunky, flamboyant right-winger Trevor Hockey, pictured at the City Ground in 1963, shortly before he was transferred to Newcastle United. As his career wore on, the much-travelled Hockey was transformed both in football style and personal appearance, the nippy flankman becoming a ball-winning midfield dynamo who forsook his quiff in favour of long hair and a beard. Hockey, a Welsh international, died at the tragically premature age of 43 in 1987 after playing in a five-a-side game in his home-town of Keighley, Yorkshire.

Fearless Frank

Centre-forward Frank Wignall plays a pass for the camera, not long after his £20,000 arrival from Everton in 1963. Big, powerful and fearless, he was a steady rather than prolific scorer for Forest throughout the middle years of the decade but he did enough to earn two England caps in 1964, bagging a brace of goals on debut against Wales at Wembley.

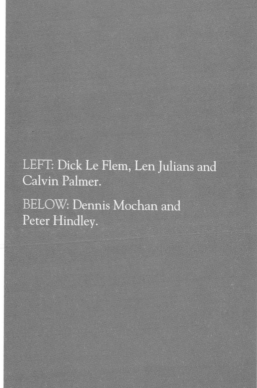

LEFT: Dick Le Flem, Len Julians and Calvin Palmer.

BELOW: Dennis Mochan and Peter Hindley.

Sign Please, Mister!

LEFT: Billy Cobb, Peter Grummitt and Johnny Quigley.

RIGHT: Henry Newton and David Pleat

BELOW: Doug Baird and Joe Wilson

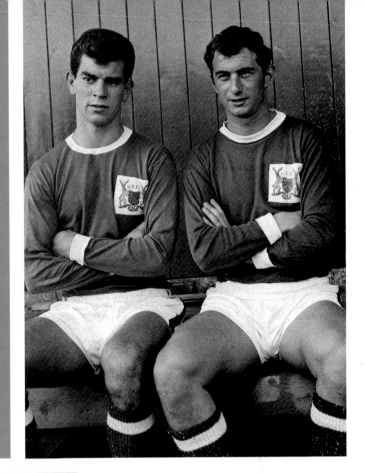

This selection of mugshots, the product of a press day at the City Ground in 1963, will reawaken echoes of childhood for many football fans who misspent part of their youth in the 1950s, '60s and '70s by snipping pictures of footballers from beloved publications such as *Charles Buchan's Football Monthly* and the weekly *Soccer Star*. Often they would be stuck into a scrapbook, then taken to a match, so the enthusiastic compiler could queue up outside the dressing rooms to ask the players to autograph their images. Ah, innocent days, long gone.

Forest striker Colin Addison is sandwiched by a pair of Spurs,
John Smith (left) and Peter Baker, in the First Division clash
at White Hart Lane in October 1963. West Countryman
Addison, a skilful operator who topped the Reds' goal charts
three times during the mid-1960s, was on target in this game.
Unfortunately Tottenham replied with four hits, three of
them by Jimmy Greaves.

Forest midfield general Jeff Whitefoot in action against Fulham's Maurice Cook at Craven Cottage in October 1963. The Londoners' own schemer, the great Johnny Haynes, is in the background.

ABOVE: Alan Hinton, the England left-winger who arrived at the City Ground from Wolves in exchange for fellow flankman Dick "Flip" Le Flem in January 1964. Hinton was quick, a beautifully accurate crosser and a dead-ball expert who packed a savage shot. However, he didn't produce his best form on a consistent basis until he moved to Derby County in 1967.

LEFT: Forest full-back Joe Wilson lunges in with a last-ditch challenge on West Ham winger Peter Brabrook at Upton Park in August 1964. The visitors, who were beginning to gel impressively in Johnny Carey's second season as manager, won the game 3-2, with Johnny Barnwell scoring twice and Alan Hinton once.

RIGHT: Johnny Barnwell, a clever attacking midfielder, signed from Arsenal for £30,000 in March 1964. He suited manager Johnny Carey's attractive, free-flowing style of play and he served Forest until the end of the decade.

Chris and Company Hammer United

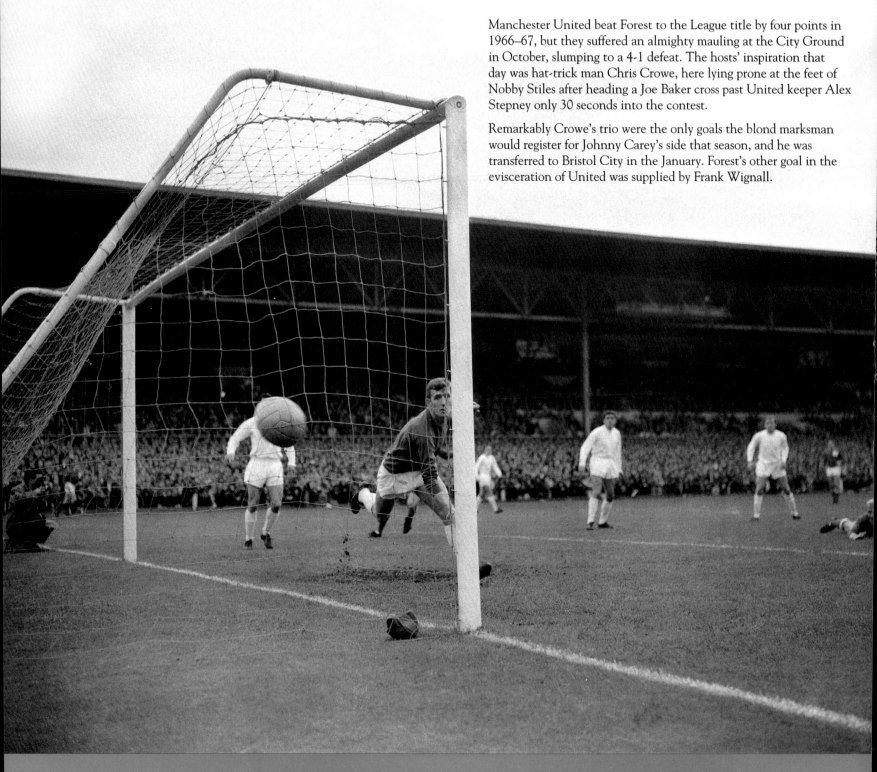

Manchester United beat Forest to the League title by four points in 1966–67, but they suffered an almighty mauling at the City Ground in October, slumping to a 4-1 defeat. The hosts' inspiration that day was hat-trick man Chris Crowe, here lying prone at the feet of Nobby Stiles after heading a Joe Baker cross past United keeper Alex Stepney only 30 seconds into the contest.

Remarkably Crowe's trio were the only goals the blond marksman would register for Johnny Carey's side that season, and he was transferred to Bristol City in the January. Forest's other goal in the evisceration of United was supplied by Frank Wignall.

With Chris Crowe excelling himself at the other end of the pitch, Forest only had to remain solid at the back to prevail over visiting title rivals Manchester United, and goalkeeper Peter Grummitt was, as usual, dependability personified. Here he rises above David Herd to punch clear from a corner, with (left to right) Johnny Barnwell and Bobby McKinlay covering on the goal-line. Bill Foulkes, on the left, is the other United attacker.

So Near, so Far

ABOVE: Johnny Carey, one of the most revered players in Manchester United history, signs autographs for fans at Old Trafford in February 1967, living up to his nickname of "Gentleman John". He returned to the scene of his former triumphs as the manager of a Forest team locked in a duel for the title with Matt Busby's Red Devils.

Bobby Charlton holds off a challenge from John Winfield to fire a shot goalwards when Forest visited Old Trafford for what, in retrospect, seems like a championship showdown. United won the game by its only goal, a typically spectacular airborne volley from Denis Law after 85 minutes. The other Forest defenders are, left to right, Henry Newton, Peter Hindley and Bobby McKinlay.

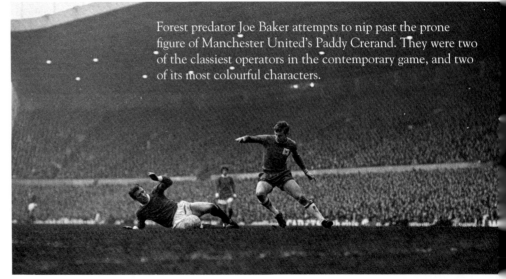

Forest predator Joe Baker attempts to nip past the prone figure of Manchester United's Paddy Crerand. They were two of the classiest operators in the contemporary game, and two of its most colourful characters.

This was rumbustious Forest centre-forward Frank Wignall in his element, soaring into aerial combat with Manchester United's iron man, centre-half Bill Foulkes.

ABOVE: Although John Winfield could be made to labour by wingers of the highest quality – Swindon Town's Don Rogers seems to have the upper hand here – fundamentally Forest's long-serving full-back, who made more than 400 senior appearances for the Reds, did a noble job in good times and bad throughout the 1960s and into the following decade. Certainly he deserved better than the moronic barracking he received from a small and mindless section of City Ground "fans" towards the end of his tenure, which led to a transfer request in 1974.

LEFT: Football fans love it when a local boy makes good, and that was the case with Henry Newton, seen here clearing Forest's lines with a powerful header while skipper Terry Hennessey looks on. Whether employed as a tenacious full-back or a workaholic midfielder, Newton was a briskly efficient, unfailingly steely operator who could consider himself unfortunate never to add full England honours to his four under-23 caps.

Like so many of his classy team-mates, he was allowed to leave the club while still in his prime, moving to Everton for £150,000 plus the services of midfielder Tommy Jackson in October 1970. Later he won a title medal with Derby County.

Trentside Trainer

Old man Hennessey, he just kept rolling along! Actually the Forest skipper, despite his receding hairline, was only 24 years old as he trained beside the River Trent ahead of the Reds' fabulously entertaining FA Cup quarter-final with Everton.

–LEGENDS–

Ian Storey-Moore·

Ian Storey-Moore was one of the most gifted footballers ever to grace the Nottingham Forest shirt. Superficially a winger, but actually a roaming raider who caused mayhem in all attacking areas, he was top scorer in five seasons out of six between 1966–67 and 1971–72. His talent was worthy of multiple international caps, but it appeared that Sir Alf Ramsey had pigeonholed the tall, strong East Anglian as a flankman, a breed employed exceedingly sparingly by the England boss following his World Cup triumph of 1966. Thus Storey-Moore had to be content with a solitary full appearance for his country, and that was a shame.

At least Forest manager Johnny Carey was thrilled by Ian's ability, and so was Brian Clough, who thought he had signed him for Derby County early in 1972, and even paraded him in front of fans before a game at the Baseball Ground, only for Manchester United to clinch a £200,000 deal.

Had Storey-Moore remained at Forest, it seems improbable that the club would have sunk so low in the early 1970s. Sadly he benefited little from his transfer to the big time, an ankle injury severely curtailing what had promised to be a glittering Old Trafford career.

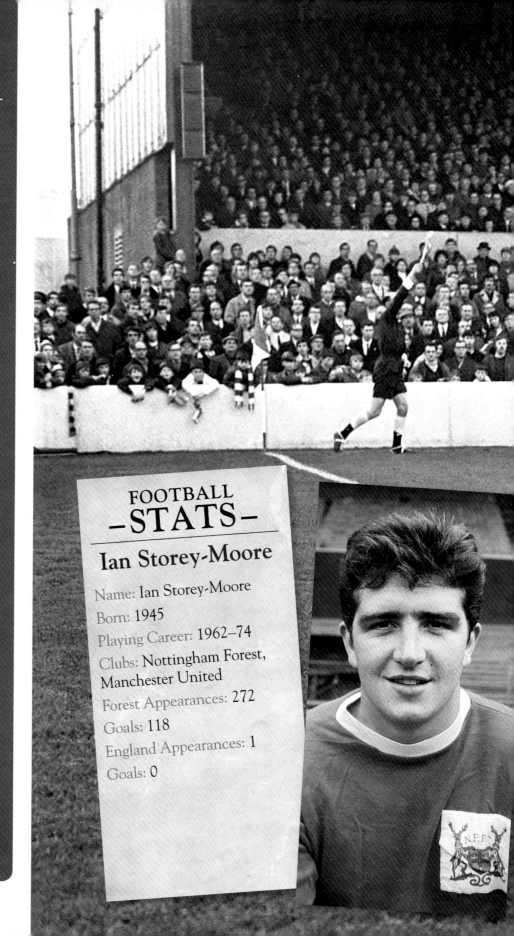

FOOTBALL –STATS–

Ian Storey-Moore

Name: Ian Storey-Moore

Born: 1945

Playing Career: 1962–74

Clubs: Nottingham Forest, Manchester United

Forest Appearances: 272

Goals: 118

England Appearances: 1

Goals: 0

Bamboozled on the byline: Ian Storey-Moore thoroughly confuses another of England's one-cap men, Chelsea's John Hollins, during the 1-1 draw between their clubs at the City Ground in November 1969.

a match in a million, the most spellbinding in living memory. At the time the Reds were going for the coveted League and FA Cup double, lying just two points behind eventual champions Manchester United with six games each to play and with home advantage in the last eight of the knockout competition.

The game started badly for Johnny Carey's men, with the much-loved striker Joe Baker being lost to injury in the first half. He was replaced by Alan Hinton, with Ian Storey-Moore switching from the left flank to centre-forward, and by the end of the afternoon that looked like a Carey masterstroke.

Everton took the lead in the first half, Storey-Moore equalized after 66 minutes, then put his side 2-1 up two minutes later. Back bounced the Toffees to level, but then in the last minute Storey-Moore nodded the winner following a nerve-janglingly dramatic sequence of action in the Everton box.

Sadly for Forest, they lost the semi-final to Spurs and could not catch United in the title race. But whenever talk turns to that riveting campaign, the City Ground faithful always have their memories of that pulsating quarter-final.

Ian Storey-Moore tucks away Forest's equalizer after Everton keeper Andy Rankin had parried a shot from Frank Wignall. 1-1.

ABOVE: Everton and England centre-half Brian Labone (right), whose accidental coming-together with Joe Baker had ended the Forest striker's season, lashes the ball away from winger Barry Lyons.

BELOW: Everton's Colin Harvey pulls off a dramatic goal-line clearance to deny Forest stopper Bobby McKinlay (not in picture), who had made a rare foray into the opposing penalty box.

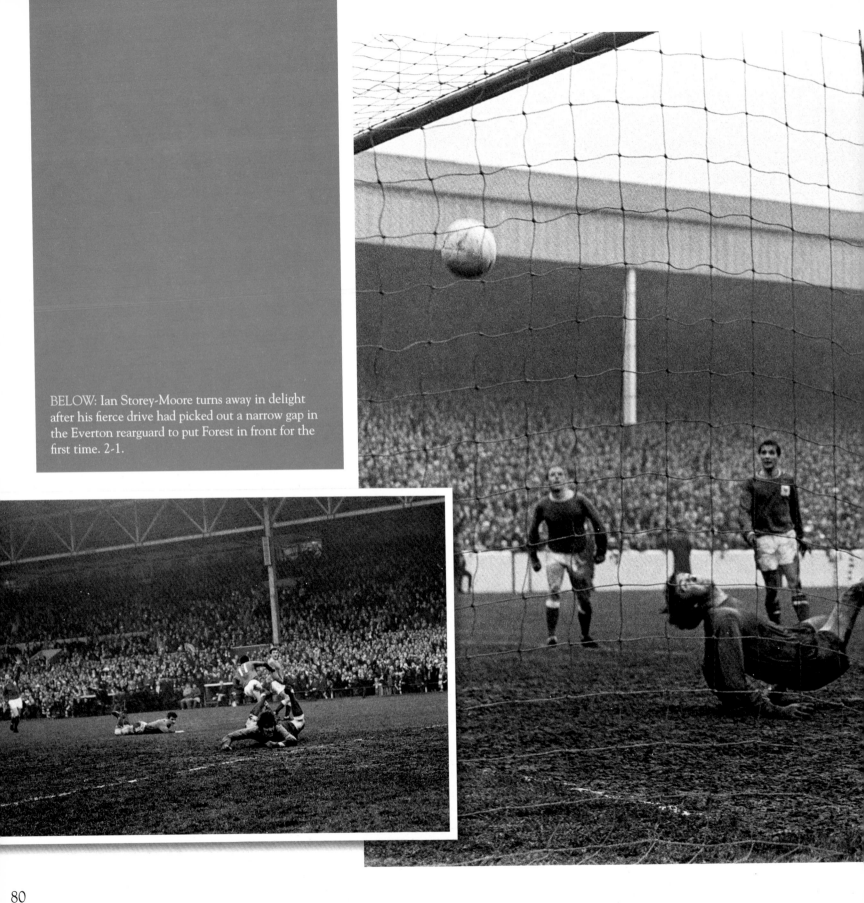

BELOW: Ian Storey-Moore turns away in delight after his fierce drive had picked out a narrow gap in the Everton rearguard to put Forest in front for the first time. 2-1.

The last-gasp winner! Having seen his first shot blocked by a defender and his second saved by keeper Andy Rankin, Ian Storey-Moore has headed against the Everton crossbar and is about to nod the rebound into the empty net to claim a place in the FA Cup semi-final as the City Ground explodes with excitement. 3-2.

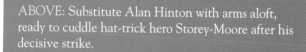
ABOVE: Substitute Alan Hinton with arms aloft, ready to cuddle hat-trick hero Storey-Moore after his decisive strike.

Joe Baker (centre) exactly where opposing defenders hated to encounter him, in a few yards of space and bearing down on the goal with the ball at his feet. Here his intended victims are Swindon Town, in an FA Cup third-round encounter at the City Ground in March

-LEGENDS-

Joe Baker

Joe Baker was a laughing cavalier of a footballer, an exuberant, audacious centre-forward, and, as an English international with a broad Scottish accent, a downright rarity.

Still only 25 when he moved to Forest from Arsenal in February 1966, he had already packed plenty into his eventful career, having averaged close to a goal per game with his first club, Hibernian, then succumbing to the lure of the lire to sign for Torino. Having experienced trauma both on and off the pitch in Italy, Baker returned to his homeland with the Gunners, for whom he also scored freely during his four terms at Highbury.

Not surprisingly it was the adventurous, attack-minded Johnny Carey who recruited Joe to the City Ground, and the swashbuckling marksman did not disappoint. In 1966–67 he was a key performer as Forest challenged for the League and FA Cup double, and his injury in the quarter-final victory over Everton was a major factor in the Reds finishing the campaign without a trophy.

When Carey's successor as manager, Matt Gillies, sold Baker to Sunderland in the summer of 1969 it provoked widespread outrage among Forest fans, who loved the Merseysider for both his entertainment value on the pitch and his engaging affability off it.

Gunned Down

LEFT: A 1-1 draw at Highbury is not usually considered a disappointing result, but Forest needed better than that in April 1967 if they were to stand a realistic chance of overhauling League leaders Manchester United in the race for the title. Here keeper Peter Grummitt foils Arsenal striker John Radford. His fellow defenders are, from the left, Bobby McKinlay, Peter Hindley and John Winfield.

BELOW: This time it's Forest's Terry Hennessey who blocks Radford's way to goal, with Arsenal's George Graham (centre) and visiting centre-half Bobby McKinlay awaiting developments.

Semi-final Frustration

Against the imposing backdrop of Hillsborough's cantilever stand, Forest spearhead Frank Wignall soars high above Spurs dreadnought Dave Mackay to deliver a header on goal during the 1967 FA Cup semi-final, but the chance went begging. Bobby McKinlay, having surged forward from defence, waits in vain for the ball to drop to him.

ABOVE: Jimmy Greaves shows a clean pair of heels to Forest right-back Peter Hindley during the FA Cup semi-final. The Tottenham maestro opened the scoring with an opportunistic left-foot daisy-cutter from 25 yards after half an hour in which the north Londoners had been decidedly second-best to Johnny Carey's team.

BELOW: Desperate defence from right-back Peter Hindley and goalkeeper Peter Grummitt as Tottenham striker Frank Saul threatens the Forest goal. Later Saul contributed the second goal of the match to put Spurs two up on their way to a 2-1 victory.

Resplendent in Nottingham Forest's change strip, skipper Terry Hennessey leads his troops into battle at Old Trafford in February 1967. His acquisition from Birmingham in November 1965 was one of the key deals of manager Johnny Carey's City Ground tenure, and when the Welsh international left to join Derby County in February 1970, he was never adequately replaced.

FOOTBALL
-STATS-

Terry Hennessey

Name: William Terence Hennessey

Born: 1942

Playing Career: 1959–73

Clubs: Birmingham City, Nottingham Forest, Derby County

Forest Appearances: 183

Goals: 6

Wales Appearances: 39

Goals: 0

-LEGENDS-

Terry Hennessey

Terry Hennessey was a composed and hugely accomplished all-round footballer, equally capable of play-making from midfield or radiating a sense of security alongside a stopper centre-half. At Forest his most effective role was in harness with Bobby McKinlay at the back, though he remained influential as an attacking force, occasionally sallying forth elegantly with the ball at his feet before dispatching a sumptuous through-pass to the likes of Joe Baker or Ian Storey-Moore.

Hennessey, an uplifting captain of both his club and his country, Wales, started his professional career with Birmingham City before joining Forest for £50,000 in November 1965. It proved to be an inspired piece of business by manager Johnny Carey, and Hennessey wielded colossal sway as Forest pushed Manchester United for the League title and reached the FA Cup semi-finals in 1966–67.

It made little sense to City Ground regulars when the Welshman was transferred to Derby County for £100,000 in February 1970 – the deal being done by Matt Gillies, Carey's replacement – especially when he flourished so grandly at the Baseball Ground, making a telling contribution as Brian Clough's side won the League championship in 1971–72.

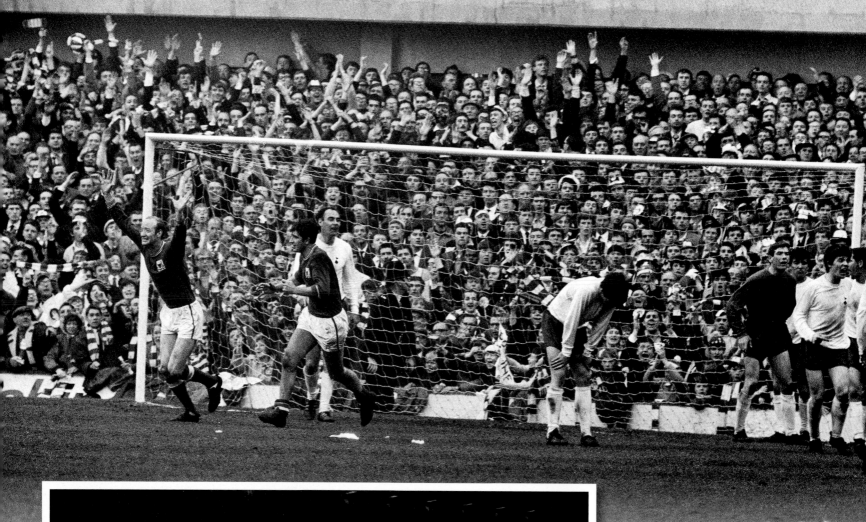

ABOVE: Terry Hennessey celebrates after frustrating the massed ranks of the Spurs defence to score in the FA Cup semi. Alas for Nottingham Forest, the Welshman's strike was merely a consolation towards the end of a 2-1 defeat.

LEFT: Forest midfielder Johnny Barnwell lunges valiantly but can't prevent Jimmy Greaves from delivering a cross during Tottenham's 2-1 FA Cup semi-final victory. Greaves relished facing Forest for the simple reason that usually he found the net against them. During his career he netted 29 times against the Reds, who suffered from his brilliant marksmanship more than any other club.

A Sad Case of "If Only"

Jim Baxter in a Sunderland shirt in December 1966, a year before his anti-climactic transfer to Nottingham Forest. "Slim Jim" had been one of the most elegantly stylish and incisively creative midfield schemers in the game during his heyday as a Glasgow Ranger, but he had under-achieved at Roker Park and his lustre had dimmed comprehensively by the time Johnny Carey gambled £100,000 in taking him to the City Ground.

Baxter's off-the-pitch excesses and his failure to adapt his strolling on-field approach as the game became quicker meant that, although he would always be an Ibrox legend, he failed to reach the pinnacles that his outrageous talent had once brought within reach. He was given a free transfer by new Forest boss Matt Gillies in 1969 and returned to Rangers, but was never again the same arrogant, irresistible force who had once made mincemeat of England at Wembley.

When Men Were Men...

No gloves, no tights, no snoods in sight as Liverpool centre-forward Ian St John (left) tussles for possession with Joe Baker, his Forest opposite number, at a snowy Anfield in February 1969. The visitors' left-winger, hoping to pick up the loose ball, is Ronnie Rees, making his debut for the club. Forest won 2-0, courtesy of a brace from Barry Lyons, but finished a disappointing 18th in the First Division table.

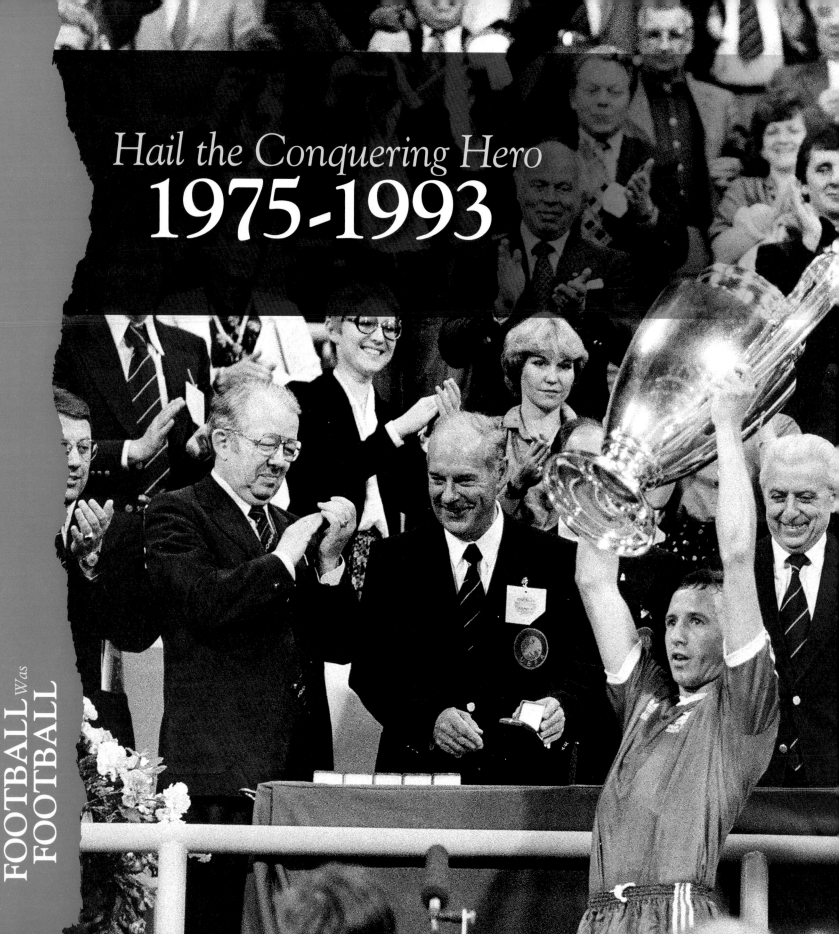

Hail the Conquering Hero
1975-1993

Nottingham Forest captain John McGovern becomes only the fourth Briton, after Billy McNeill, Bobby Charlton and Emlyn Hughes, to be presented with the European Cup, following the victory over Malmö in the Olympic Stadium, Munich, in the spring of 1979. Waiting in line behind him, and itching for a touch of the silverware, are Larry Lloyd and Frank Clark.

1975 Brian Clough is the new manager. **1977** Third in second tier, promoted again. **1978** Forest are League champions for the only time in their history; also win League Cup for first time, beating Liverpool 1-0 in final, and reach last eight of FA Cup. **1979** Forest win the European Cup, beating Malmö 1-0; retain League Cup, beating Southampton 3-2 at Wembley; runners up to Liverpool in First Division. **1980** Forest are Kings of Europe again, this time defeating Hamburg 1-0 in final; League Cup final reverse against Wolves. **1981** FA Cup quarter-finalists. **1984** Clough's men finish third in First Division, their highest for five seasons. **1988** Another third place, quarter-finals of FA Cup. **1989** A third League Cup triumph, beating Luton 3-1 in final; yet another third place in title battle; Hillsborough tragedy and defeat to Liverpool in restarted FA Cup semi-final. **1990** Forest taste League Cup glory for the fourth time, overcoming Oldham 1-0 at Wembley. **1991** Reds lose FA Cup final to Spurs. **1992** Forest reach their sixth League Cup final, losing to Manchester United. **1993** Brian Clough retires; Forest relegated from the Premier League as bottom club.

Move Over Liverpool...

For all the genuine uplift during the eras of Billy Walker and Johnny Carey, nothing had prepared the loyal supporters of Nottingham Forest for the sheer ecstasy that was coming their way during the sensational reign of one Brian Clough.

Until he breezed into the City Ground, radiating self-belief and jolting all sorts of folk with his unorthodox approach, Forest had been a medium-sized provincial club which might enjoy the occasional success but was simply not programmed for a sustained assault on the most glittering prizes the game had to offer – in this country and beyond!

Soon Clough transformed the football landscape, first leading Forest into the top grade, then knocking all-powerful Liverpool off their perch, all as a prelude to dominating Europe for two unforgettable seasons.

More triumphs followed before his light dimmed, but whatever barbs fate might hold for Forest fans in the future, they would always have their unperishable memories of the astonishing Cloughie and all his works.

Champs in Waiting

The Nottingham Forest squad with which Brian Clough faced the prospect of top-flight football in the late summer of 1977. Most pundits thought they might struggle in the wake of their last-gasp promotion, but the Boss had a trick or two up his sleeve.

Back row, left to right: Jimmy Gordon (trainer), Bryn Gunn, Martin O'Neill, Ian Bowyer, Peter Withe, Viv Anderson, John Middleton, Garry Birtles, Barry Butlin, Colin Barrett, Kenny Burns, Brian Clough (manager). Front row: Larry Lloyd, Sean Haslegrave, Frank Clark, John McGovern, John Robertson, Terry Curran, Tony Woodcock.

Enter the Messiah

A young man named Brian Clough arrives for work, complete with Mercedes, on his first day at the City Ground on 6th January 1975. Nottingham Forest would never be the same again.

ABOVE: "Hello gentlemen, meet the future. One day this little boy will be your centre-forward." Those might have been the words as the new Forest boss introduces his son, Nigel, to his directors. Meanwhile the manager's other son, Simon, is content to remain in the background.

Four Faces of a Footballing Mastermind

Brian Clough was not shy at posing for the camera after taking the Nottingham Forest job. Here he displays the familiar confident grin, soundbite at the ready (left), the serious man with a point to make (below), the intensely focused all-round sportsman on the tennis court (opposite above) and the riverbank thinker, already plotting Forest's future by the side of the Trent (opposite below).

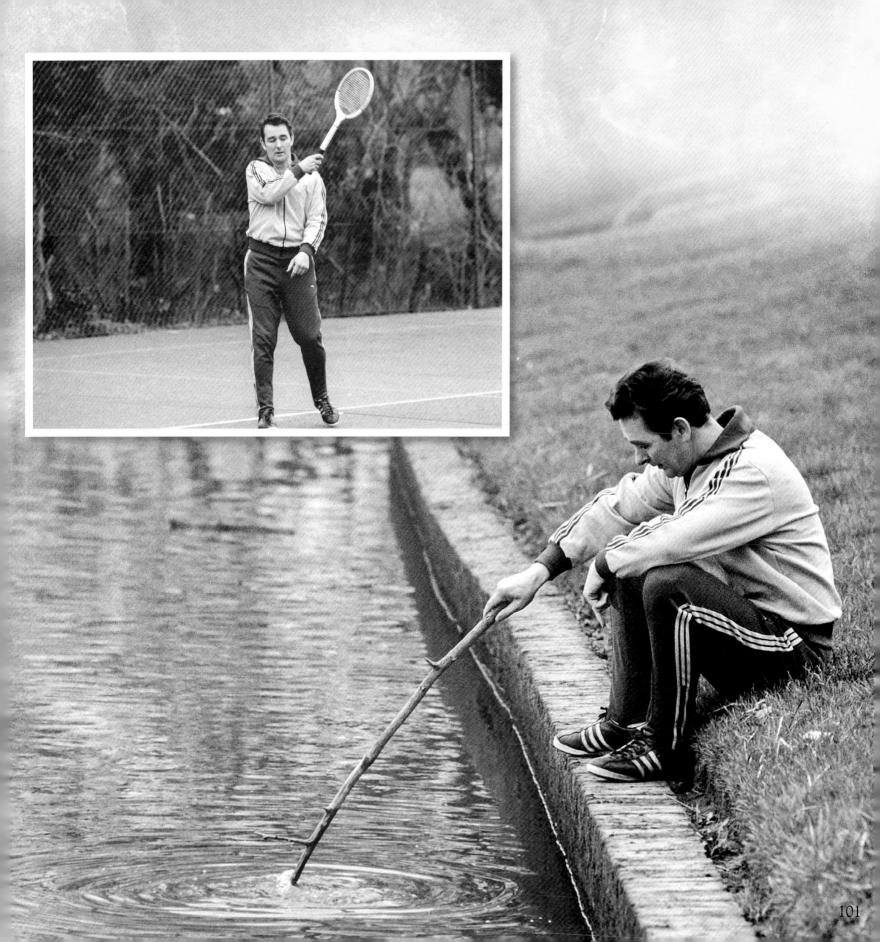

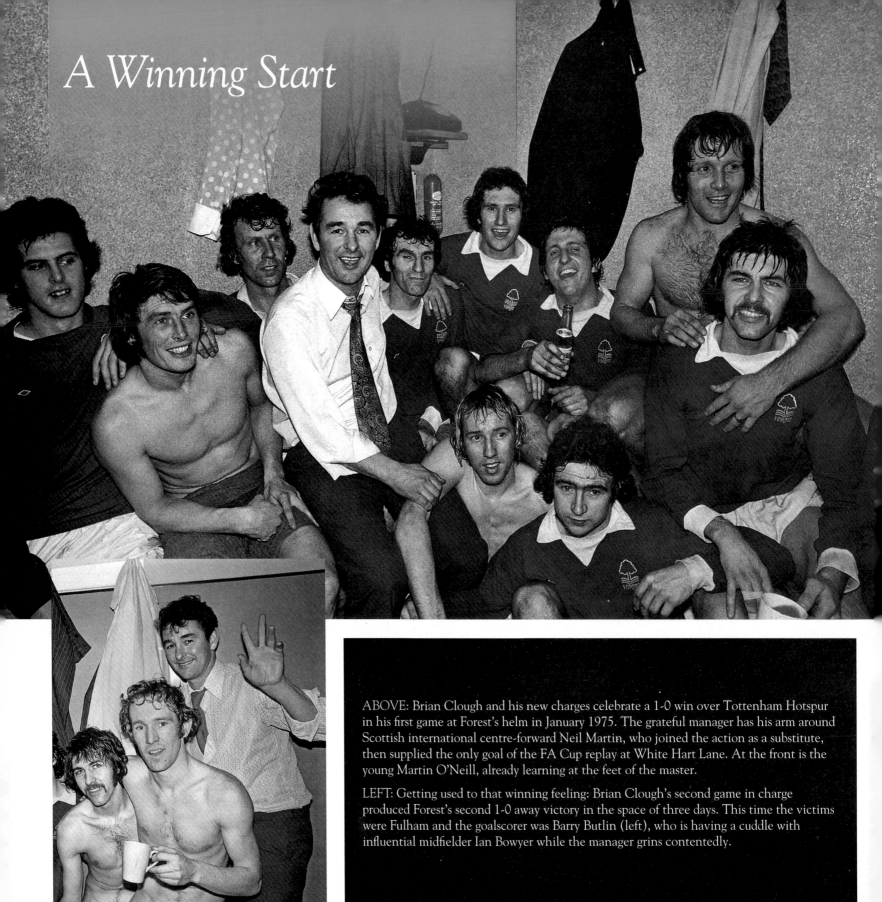

A Winning Start

ABOVE: Brian Clough and his new charges celebrate a 1-0 win over Tottenham Hotspur in his first game at Forest's helm in January 1975. The grateful manager has his arm around Scottish international centre-forward Neil Martin, who joined the action as a substitute, then supplied the only goal of the FA Cup replay at White Hart Lane. At the front is the young Martin O'Neill, already learning at the feet of the master.

LEFT: Getting used to that winning feeling: Brian Clough's second game in charge produced Forest's second 1-0 away victory in the space of three days. This time the victims were Fulham and the goalscorer was Barry Butlin (left), who is having a cuddle with influential midfielder Ian Bowyer while the manager grins contentedly.

LEFT: Forest's George Lyall tries to get a toe-end to the ball, but Fulham's Bobby Moore, calmness personified as ever, sees the leather safely into the hands of his goalkeeper Peter Mellor during the FA Cup fourth-round third replay at the City Ground in February 1975. Forest lost 2-1, bowing out of the competition after six games, four of which had been drawn.

BELOW: "Welcome to Nottingham, lads. You'll fit in perfectly here." So might Forest boss Brian Clough have greeted his two new signings, John McGovern (left) and John O'Hare in February 1975 – and he would have been bang on in his assessment. He knew the duo immensely well, having managed McGovern at Hartlepools, Derby and Leeds, and had charge of O'Hare at both the Baseball Ground and Elland Road. Both men had helped him to lift silverware along the A52 at Derby, and now they would do so at the City Ground, too.

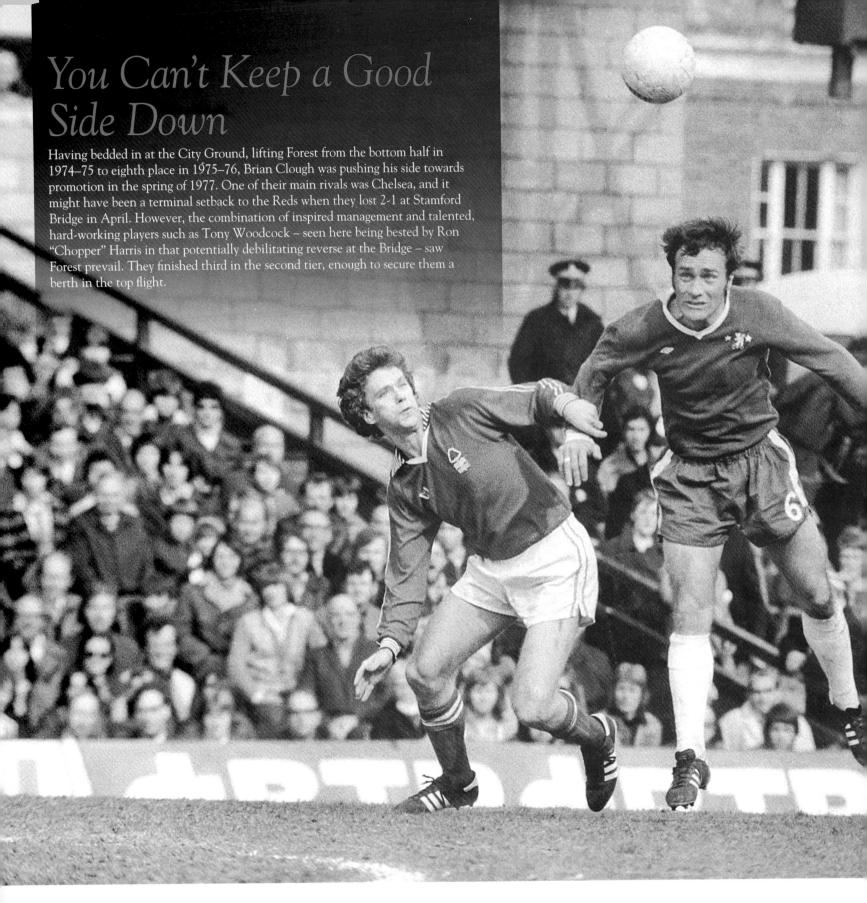

You Can't Keep a Good Side Down

Having bedded in at the City Ground, lifting Forest from the bottom half in 1974–75 to eighth place in 1975–76, Brian Clough was pushing his side towards promotion in the spring of 1977. One of their main rivals was Chelsea, and it might have been a terminal setback to the Reds when they lost 2-1 at Stamford Bridge in April. However, the combination of inspired management and talented, hard-working players such as Tony Woodcock – seen here being bested by Ron "Chopper" Harris in that potentially debilitating reverse at the Bridge – saw Forest prevail. They finished third in the second tier, enough to secure them a berth in the top flight.

ABOVE: Big Peter Withe soars above his Chelsea opposite number, Steve Finnieston, during the 2-1 defeat by Eddie McCreadie's side in west London. On the left is Withe's strike partner Tony Woodcock, with whom he gelled ideally, the pair a classic combination of a towering target man and a nippier, more skilful foil.

BELOW: Forest's unobtrusively excellent John McGovern takes on Chelsea's more silkily skilful Ray Wilkins (right) in a midfield confrontation of contrasting types.

Forest on the Rise

Peter Withe (fourth from the left) grins in exultation, and maybe a tinge of relief, to see the ball cross Plymouth Argyle's goal-line during Forest's crucial 2-1 victory at Home Park in the penultimate game of their 1976–77 promotion campaign. Withe and Tony Woodcock both hit the target that day in Devon, and although neither managed to score in their final game of the season, an own goal by Millwall defender Jon Moore at the City Ground proved enough to secure Forest a place in the top flight.

THE "ALL★STAR" PETROL CARD CO. ·272

The Brains Trust behind the golden era awaiting Forest in the autumn of 1977. Showing varying degrees of animation on the bench at Loftus Road during the 2-0 win over Queen's Park Rangers – Ian Bowyer and Kenny Burns supplied the goals – are trainer Jimmy Meadows, manager Brian Clough and assistant boss Peter Taylor.

Clash of the Titans

LEFT: Nineteen-year-old Chris Woods, Forest's hero in both League Cup final encounters with Liverpool in March 1978, directs his elders where to run. Woods, who would never play a League game for Brian Clough but would go on to collect 43 England caps while serving other clubs, was only in the side because Peter Shilton was Cup-tied, but if the Scousers imagined that the rookie might prove a weak link, they had another think coming.

It was principally down to Woods that the first game, at Wembley, finished goalless, as Woods defied Kenny Dalglish and company time and again with a series of fabulous saves. Then in the Old Trafford replay he stood tall again, holding firm as Liverpool pressed relentlessly, leaving John Robertson to secure victory with the only goal of the game from the penalty spot. Thus the Scottish winger earned his share of the glory, but nobody deserved a winner's medal more than the valiant Chris Woods.

ABOVE: When warriors collide: Liverpool's Jimmy Case tries an ambitious overhead while Kenny Burns of Forest stands his ground, with Frank Clark as a handy reinforcement, in the League Cup final at Wembley in March 1978. For once, the secondary domestic Cup competition was being contested by the two best teams in the land that spring.

LEFT: Brian Clough and his centre-forward, Peter Withe, after Liverpool have been beaten in the League Cup final replay. For them the season's most crucial business still lay ahead – the successful chase for the League title that would confound the critics.

BELOW: The spoils of victory. Forest skipper John McGovern shows off the League Cup to the City Ground faithful ahead of their First Division meeting with Newcastle United in March 1978. It was Forest's first major trophy since winning the FA Cup in 1959, but there was no hint of complacency. An hour later McGovern and company got straight back down to business, beating the Magpies 2-0 courtesy of a John Robertson penalty and a goal from Viv Anderson.

Forest stars celebrate with the League Cup. Left to right are Tony Woodcock, Martin O'Neill, Kenny Burns, John Robertson and Larry Lloyd. The final, replayed at Old Trafford, was clinched by a controversial John Robertson penalty which Liverpool claimed vehemently should never have been given. They reckoned that when Phil Thompson downed John O'Hare early in the second half, the foul took place marginally outside the box – and television replays proved them right. But a glance at the record book reveals that Forest won 1-0, and that was all that mattered to Clough and company on an emotional night in Manchester.

That Title Feeling

Goals win championships, but so do saves, as Peter Shilton demonstrated by tipping this bullet header from Coventry City's Mick Ferguson over the bar in the goalless draw at Highfield Road in April 1978. It clinched the first, and still the only, League crown in Forest's history, with four games to spare. To reach the ball the England goalkeeper had to change direction at the last moment, then fly through the air with arm outstretched, and he rated his effort one of the best of his career.

LEFT: With the League title safely in the bag, Brian Clough and his assistant Peter Taylor celebrate with cups of tea in the Coventry City dressing room. Theirs had been an incredible achievement, because when Forest had been promoted a year earlier many pundits had predicted a rapid return to the second tier. Yet they took the First Division by storm, losing only three games, all in the first half of the season, then sweeping to the top domestic prize with an extraordinary sequence of 26 League matches without defeat. The run was extended to a then-record 42 games in the following autumn.

The sight of Nottingham Forest brandishing silverware became a familiar one during the late 1970s. Here are Clough and Taylor's increasingly confident troops with the Charity Shield after thrashing FA Cup holders Ipswich Town 5-0 at Wembley in August 1978. Back row, left to right: David Needham, Ian Bowyer, Colin Barrett, Viv Anderson, Martin O'Neill (two goals), Peter Shilton, Larry Lloyd (one goal), Peter Withe (one goal), Archie Gemmill. Front row: Kenny Burns, Tony Woodcock, John McGovern and John Robertson (one goal).

FOOTBALL -STATS-

Tony Woodcock

Name: Anthony Stewart Woodcock

Born: 1955

Playing Career: 1974–86

Clubs: Nottingham Forest, Lincoln City on loan, Doncaster Rovers on loan, Cologne, Arsenal, Fortuna

Forest Appearances: 180

Goals: 62

England Appearances: 42

Goals: 16

ABOVE: Tony Woodcock attempts to shake off a marker in the European Cup quarter-final clash with Grasshoppers Zurich at the City Ground in March 1979.

Tony Woodcock (left) and his partner in goals Garry Birtles, after sinking Southampton in the 1979 League Cup final. Woodcock scored once and Birtles twice in the Forest's 3-2 victory.

—LEGENDS—

Tony Woodcock

When Brian Clough dispatched Tony Woodcock on loan to Lincoln City, then Doncaster Rovers, in the mid-1970s, the Nottingham-born centre-forward appeared to be on his way out of Forest permanently. But then came unexpected opportunity and thrilling displays in the Anglo-Scottish Cup, and suddenly Woodcock was a key man in earning promotion from the second flight in 1977.

Thereafter his career gained spectacular momentum as he helped to lift the League title, the European Cup and two League Cups, as well as being voted PFA Young Player of the Year for 1977–78, before being transferred to Cologne in November 1979.

Woodcock was a lovely footballer to watch but the very devil to mark. He was blessed with scorching pace, adhesive ball control, the knack of worming past defenders in a confined space and sharp reflexes in front of the net. He forged two major partnerships at the City Ground, first with Peter Withe and then with Garry Birtles, excelling alongside both men.

He won his first England caps during his Forest days, the majority when he was in Germany and the final handful having joined Arsenal, for whom he became the leading scorer of the 1980s.

–LEGENDS–

Viv Anderson

Viv Anderson was that cherished rarity, a thoroughly entertaining full-back. The flamboyant local lad, who went on to serve Arsenal and Manchester United but never topped his superb achievements with his home-town club, cut a particularly swashbuckling figure as he sprinted into attack, his characteristic elastic stride carrying him beyond all but the paciest of opponents. But a full-back's primary concern is defending, and Anderson shone in that department, too, often snaking out a long right leg to make a saving challenge just when it seemed his winger had left him for dead.

Beyond that, Viv possessed two other attributes particularly beloved of Brian Clough and, later, Alex Ferguson – a burning hatred of losing that was bone-deep, and a frenetic commitment to see that such a disaster happened only when the last drop of energy had been expended.

Anderson, the first black footballer to win a full England cap, contributed colossally to the silverware avalanche that engulfed the City Ground trophy room during Clough's first decade at the club. He was sold to Arsenal for £250,000 in 1984, striking up a classy full-back partnership with England colleague Kenny Sansom. Then came Old Trafford and several more clubs, his enthusiasm burning as brightly to the last as it did on his first day with the Forest.

Viv Anderson

Name: Vivian Alexander Anderson

Born: 1956

Playing Career: 1974–95

Clubs: Nottingham Forest, Arsenal, Manchester United, Sheffield Wednesday, Barnsley, Middlesbrough

Forest Appearances: 430

Goals: 22

England Appearances: 30

Goals: 2

Managerial Career: Barnsley

Forest's Viv Anderson polices Kenny Dalglish of Liverpool during the goalless draw at the City Ground in April 1981.

Knocking Liverpool Off Another Perch

Forest defenders Frank Clark (centre) and Kenny Burns (right) might be sighing with relief as goalkeeper Peter Shilton gathers the ball to frustrate another Liverpool attack at Anfield in the second leg of the two great sides' titanic European Cup first-round clash at Anfield in September 1978.

Bob Paisley's men were holders of the trophy, but their grip is about to be loosened. Forest won 2-0 in the first leg at the City Ground, thanks to strikes from Garry Birtles and Colin Barrett, and this game finished goalless.

ABOVE: It's impossible to tell from the expressions of Forest's Tony Woodcock and Alan Kennedy of Liverpool who has won and who has lost as the two England internationals leave the Anfield pitch at the end of their European Cup first-round second-leg encounter. In fact, it was Forest who would be continuing their continental adventure, while the Merseysiders, champions of Europe for the previous two years, were now free to concentrate on recapturing the League title from Brian Clough's men.

Who would have thought it? The elevation of Kenny Burns to Footballer of the Year in the spring of 1978 exemplified the fairytale rise of Nottingham Forest from second-tier nonentities into the finest team in the country

Kenny Burns

The genius of the Clough-Taylor managerial combo was rarely illustrated more compellingly than by the case of Kenny Burns. The cocksure Scot was one of the roughest diamonds in the Football League as a striker-cum-occasional midfielder with Birmingham City throughout the early and middle 1970s.

But then Taylor convinced Clough that he needed him at Forest – as central-defensive partner to Larry Lloyd. At that point the abrasive Burns had experienced multiple disciplinary problems, had never played at centre-half in his life, and had just completed a hugely successful top-flight campaign as the Blues' principal spearhead, netting 19 times in 36 outings.

Clough trusted Taylor to the tune of a £150,000 investment, Burns duly slotted into a formidable defensive triangle with Lloyd and Peter Shilton, and Forest scaled virtually every pinnacle in the game. Along the way the rugged Glaswegian demonstrated, too, that he was by no means merely a kicker, revealing hitherto unsuspected sophistication as a passer and an intelligent reader of the game.

Such was his new status that in 1978 Burns was named Footballer of the Year and went to Argentina as part of the Scotland World Cup squad. His £400,000 transfer to Leeds United in October 1981 was deeply regretted by the majority of Forest fans.

FOOTBALL -STATS-

Kenny Burns

Name: Kenneth Burns

Born: 1953

Playing Career: 1971–86

Clubs: Birmingham City, Nottingham Forest, Leeds United, Derby County, Notts County on loan, Barnsley

Forest Appearances: 196

Goals: 15

Scotland Appearances: 20

Goals: 1

ABOVE: "Just do what I say, young man, and I'll make a star of you!" If Brian Clough ever made that promise to Kenny Burns, he kept it to the letter. The rugged Scot was prominent as Clough inspired his Forest side to scale the loftiest pinnacles both in England and in Europe.

Goals Galore on European Trail

Sharpshooters Garry Birtles (left) and Tony Woodcock sprint towards the left touchline to celebrate with arch-creator John Robertson, who has just laid on a typical pinpoint cross for Woodcock to nod Forest's second goal in their 5-1 European Cup evisceration of AEK Athens at the City Ground in November 1978.

The AEK Athens defenders had no answer to the mesmeric skills of Scottish international left-winger John Robertson as Forest cruised into the third round of the European Cup in November 1978, their 5-1 City Ground triumph completing a 6-1 aggregate rout of the Greeks.

Garry Birtles whacks a left-foot scorcher towards the AEK Athens goal during Forest's comprehensive European Cup triumph at the City Ground. Birtles was a dashing front-runner who, on his day, could unhinge the most clamlike of rearguards with his incisive approach, and he formed a potent dual spearhead with Tony Woodcock.

Forest Make Swiss Roll

Garry Birtles readies himself for some near-post action as the Grasshoppers Zurich defence prepares to repel a Forest corner in the first leg of the European Cup quarter-final at the City Ground in March 1979. The other Reds attacker is centre-half David Needham, who often caused havoc in opposing penalty boxes with his powerful heading ability, contributing 13 goals during his City Ground tenure.

ABOVE: Forest's Scottish midfield maestro Archie Gemmill bewitches a pair of Grasshoppers defenders in the City Ground mud during the European Cup last-eight clash in March 1979. Although only just short of his 32nd birthday, the diminutive schemer was still in his creative prime, his cocktail of dynamism and courage, intelligence and pure skill proving a colossal factor in Forest's progress to the semi-finals. However, Brian Clough didn't pick him for the final against Malmö, and he was freed to join Birmingham City in the following August.

BELOW: John Robertson sends Swiss goalkeeper Berbig the wrong way as he dispatches a perfect penalty to put Forest 2-1 in front early in the second half against Grasshoppers Zurich in the first leg of the European Cup quarter-final. Sulser had opened the scoring for the visitors, but Garry Birtles had equalized, then Archie Gemmill and Larry Lloyd massaged the scoreline with two late goals. The Reds prevailed 5-2 on aggregate.

League Cup Retained

ABOVE: All the joy of a Wembley scorer is encapsulated by the leaping Garry Birtles, about to be engulfed by the arms of John Robertson. Birtles grabbed a brace on the way to a 3-2 League Cup final triumph over Southampton in 1979.

LEFT: Former Forest winger Terry Curran (left) does his utmost to evade the typically vigorous challenge of Archie Gemmill during the 1979 League Cup final. The tenacious Gemmill never knew when he was beaten and had been one of the most effective midfielders in the land throughout the 1970s, first for Derby County, then with the Reds. Austin Hayes is the Southampton man on the right.

BELOW: Forest stopper David Needham attempts to hook the ball away from Southampton striker Phil Boyer at Wembley.

–LEGENDS–

Martin O'Neill

Martin O'Neill's Forest career had lost impetus and he was on the transfer list when Brian Clough replaced Allan Brown as manager in January 1975. The bright young Irishman, who turned his back on a career in law to play football, had made a promising start after his arrival from Distillery in October 1971, but now it seemed he might have made the wrong decision.

Enter Clough, who didn't always see eye to eye with O'Neill, but recognized his value as a dynamic presence on the right side of midfield. He was a vital cog as Forest rose from the Second Division in 1977, then performed even more impressively alongside Archie Gemmill as the League championship was lifted in 1978.

Unsurprisingly O'Neill was unhappy to be omitted from the 1979 European Cup final – Clough believed he wasn't fully fit, though the player maintained that he was fine – but there was rich consolation when he helped to defeat Hamburg when the trophy was retained a year later.

Forest's most-capped player until his 36 appearances for Northern Ireland while at the club was passed by Stuart Pearce for England, O'Neill fell out of favour with his acerbic boss during 1980–81 and made a surprise exit, joining Norwich City. Later O'Neill became a successful, and sometimes controversial, manager in his own right.

Martin O'Neill controls the ball while evading the attention of Southampton's David Peach in the 1979 League Cup final at Wembley.

Martin O'Neill is challenged by the lunging Kenny Hibbitt of Wolves in the 1980 League Cup final. Though Forest's industrious Irishman displayed all his customary commitment, and the Reds enjoyed the lion's share of possession, that was not enough to avert a 1-0 Wolves victory.

FOOTBALL
–STATS–

Martin O'Neill

Name: Martin Hugh Michael O'Neill

Born: 1952

Playing Career: 1971–85

Clubs: Distillery, Nottingham Forest, Norwich City, Manchester City, Notts County

Forest Appearances: 371

Goals: 62

Northern Ireland Appearances: 64

Goals: 8

Managerial Career: Wycombe Wanderers, Norwich City, Leicester City, Celtic, Aston Villa, Sunderland

In Sight of the Pinnacle

ABOVE: Long-time followers of Forest and the wider football family alike had to pinch themselves to believe it, but the legend on the pennant in John McGovern's hand offers proof that the Reds had reached the semi-final of the world's most prestigious club competition.

The City Ground, replete with more than 40,000 fans, Forest's biggest crowd of the 1978–79 European Cup campaign, was rocking for this first leg against Cologne, for whom their captain, West German international Bernhard Cullmann, was doing the honours.

LEFT: Forest's midfield general Archie Gemmill looked characteristically perky and creative in the early going at home to Cologne, but the West Germans took a potentially crushing two-goal early advantage, and soon Gemmill was injured.

He was replaced by Frank Clark, who slotted into defence with Ian Bowyer moving forward into midfield, and the new formation worked wonders. Garry Birtles nodded Forest back into contention, Bowyer levelled with a low drive and John Robertson, with a rare diving header, put the hosts in front with half an hour to go. Alas, a speculative shot from Japanese substitute Yasuhiko Okudera somehow found its way under the body of the diving Shilton, making the final score 3-3.

LEFT: Ian Bowyer takes on a posse of Cologne opponents early in the City Ground draw. He made a crucial contribution by scoring Forest's second goal, but it was his climactic strike in the return leg, a 65th-minute header after Garry Birtles had flicked on a corner from John Robertson, which made Bowyer a hero of the ages. It was the only goal of the game, and it put Nottingham Forest into the final of the European Cup.

BELOW: The glum demeanour of defenders Colin Barrett (left) and David Needham, as they trudge off through the City Ground mud at the end of the 3-3 draw with Cologne in the first leg of the European Cup semi-final summed up the general mood among Forest fans. With three away goals in the bag – they would count double in the event if a draw – the West Germans were clearly the warmest of favourites for the return encounter. But although the Reds had played poorly in front of their own supporters, they were not done yet.

CHAMPIONS OF EUROPE

Sheer Quality

LEFT: Trevor Francis swerves past a Malmö defender in the 1979 European Cup final at the Olympic Stadium in Munich. The softly spoken Devonian, subject of the first £1 million transfer between British clubs when he joined Forest from Birmingham City in February that year, was playing his first game in the world's top club competition.

BELOW: Trevor Francis makes the most impressive down-payment imaginable on his £1 million fee by scoring the only goal of the 1979 European Cup final. Shortly before half-time John Robertson delivered a trademark cross from the left and Francis, lurking slightly beyond the far post, lunged forward to head the ball powerfully, high into the net fractionally inside the upright, comfortably beyond the reach of plunging Malmö goalkeeper Jan Moller. There never seemed any likelihood of a Swedish comeback. As Brian Clough said later of that decisive moment: "One-nil. Pass me the European Cup. Thank you!"

Viv Anderson outpaces a Malmö raider to snuff out an attack from the Swedish underdogs in the European Cup final. The pacy, skilful, hyper-competitive England right-back gave a typically immaculate display, but never came under much pressure from a Malmö side so weakened by the absence of some half a dozen regulars that manager Bobby Houghton had to fill the central-defensive positions with midfielders.

Tony Woodcock fires a left-foot shot towards the Malmö goal but was frustrated for the umpteenth time on the night. Despite utterly dominating the game, Forest could not underline their superiority with more goals, which meant the outcome was in doubt until the final whistle.

Garry Birtles finds space for a left-foot scorcher, but the Malmö goal survived. Still, as he clutched his winner's medal later in the evening, the former carpet-fitter who had joined Forest from non-League Long Eaton for a mere £2,000 in December 1976, could congratulate himself on a glorious European Cup campaign in which he had contributed six goals, netting in every round except the final.

Man Who Scored the Golden Goal

LEFT: Trevor Francis brandishes the spoils of victory after his header had earned victory in the 1979 European Cup final against Malmö in Munich. Although he played fewer than a century of games for Nottingham Forest before leaving for Manchester City in September 1981, he had inscribed his name indelibly in the club's folklore. Francis was unlucky with injuries during his two-and-a-half-year City Ground sojourn, but still managed to deliver 37 goals.

BELOW: Brian Clough might have once called him a lazy slob, but now John Robertson – arguably the greatest Nottingham Forest footballer of all time – has his hands on the most prized bauble in the club game after setting up the goal that beat Malmö for Trevor Francis.

The Fairytale is Complete

Only some 27 months after languishing in eighth place in the Second Division, Nottingham Forest are champions of Europe. Partying beside the pitch at Munich's Olympic Stadium after beating Malmö are, standing left to right, Viv Anderson, Peter Shilton, sub Chris Woods, John McGovern, Ian Bowyer, sub David Needham, trainer Jimmy Gordon, Trevor Francis, Frank Clark (nearly hidden) and sub John O'Hare. Crouching are Larry Lloyd, John Robertson, Tony Woodcock and Garry Birtles with Kenny Burns in a headlock.

A vivid contrast in the expressions of Nottingham Forest's management team in the hour of their greatest glory. Peter Taylor, fist aloft, grins exultantly, while Brian Clough, at least at the moment the camera shutter clicked, is markedly solemn.

Perhaps the Boss was rueing the fact that it had been such a lacklustre final, but that was hardly Forest's fault given that their opponents had defended in such stultifying depth.

LEFT: The game itself might have been an anti-climax, and even some of the triumphant Forest players confessed that the dressing-room atmosphere after beating an unenterprising Malmö side was a trifle flat, but taking the European Cup on a lap of honour around the Olympic Stadium, Munich, was still a magical process for Tony Woodcock (left) and Larry Lloyd.

RIGHT: Keeper Peter Shilton (left) and goal-scorer Trevor Francis take their turn in the silverware parade. Shilton had little to do in the final against Malmö, and had performed below his customary impeccable standard in the 3-3 semi-final first-leg draw with Cologne, but he had ensured Forest booked their Munich place with a wonder save in the dying seconds of the second leg.

135

Big Larry Lloyd, here chasing the ball watched by team-mate Viv Anderson (left) in Forest's 4-1 home win over his previous club, Coventry City, in August 1979, cut a formidable figure on a football pitch. He started his career with his home-town club, Bristol Rovers, then became Ron Yeats' replacement at the heart of the Liverpool defence. But after tasting League title and UEFA Cup glory, and making his full England debut, the strapping stopper saw his star decline at Anfield. Next came a lacklustre spell at Coventry, which was ended when Brian Clough signed him for a knockdown £60,000 in 1976. There followed a rousing resurrection at the City Ground, encompassing not only another League title but also two European Cup successes and a brief return to the international stage, before he finished his playing days with Wigan Athletic.

Decades later Martin O'Neill and Liverpool's Alan Hansen, here towering over the fallen Forest midfielder, would prove amusingly combative sparring partners as pundits in a television studio, but here they are in their playing pomp as the Merseysiders visited the City Ground for the first leg of the League Cup semi-final in January 1980. This meeting of the eloquent duo ended with O'Neill marginally the happier, with Forest prevailing 1-0, courtesy of a John Robertson penalty. Holding a watching brief are Liverpool's Phil Thompson (left) and goalkeeper Ray Clemence, who is being hounded by the hosts' Ian Bowyer. The second leg finished 1-1, so Brian Clough's men won 2-1 on aggregate.

ABOVE: Peter Shilton …
around 1,400 senior appearances,
125 caps for England and, as a
Nottingham Forest player, two
European Cups and the League
title. Some player!

RIGHT: Peter Shilton at his
most majestic, flying through the
air to repel a shot that had been
apparently destined for the top
corner of his net. Brian Clough
reckoned a good goalkeeper
could save a team 18 points a
season – and Shilton was a great
goalkeeper, the most dominant of
his era.

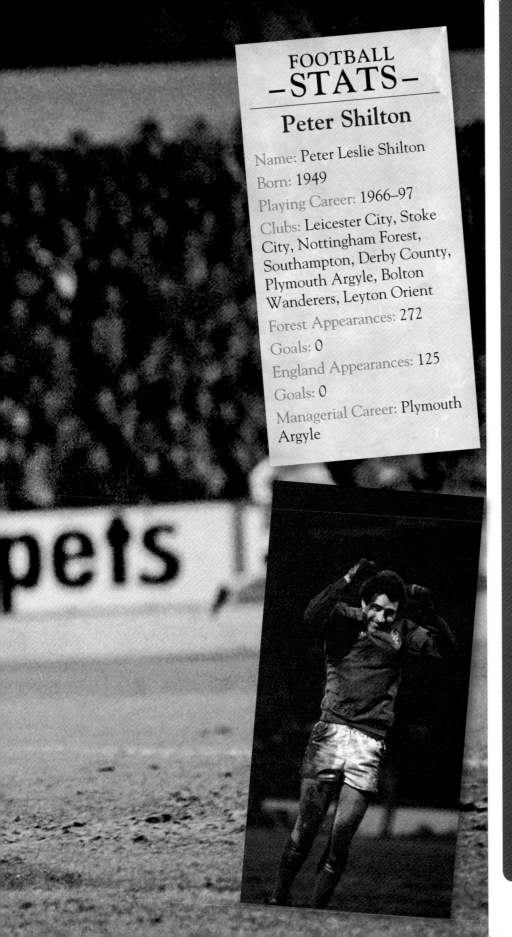

-LEGENDS-

Peter Shilton

Brian Clough recruited the best goalkeeper in the world – and one of the finest of all time – when he signed Peter Shilton from Stoke City in September 1977 for £250,000, then the biggest ever fee for a last line of defence. Still, in retrospect it was staggering that Clough was allowed to get his hands on Shilton, given that the likes of big-spending Manchester United were in the market for a keeper.

Shilton was special, boasting every attribute needed for his craft. He was a big man, and appeared to grow even more colossal as he took his stance between the posts, making the goal practically disappear in the eyes of opposing marksmen.

But there was rather more to the burly Midlander than that. He was phenomenally agile, as brave as a gladiator, he was as adept at plucking crosses from the air as he was at pouching shots, and he was utterly brilliant positionally, possessing an instinctive appreciation of angles. Clearly he must have been a paragon for his first club, Leicester City, to allow the great Gordon Banks to leave so the rookie could take over.

At Forest Shilton was central to all the club's headiest achievements, then he went on to total a record 125 England caps – the figure would have been even more remarkable but for the presence of his excellent contemporary Ray Clemence – and to top 1,000 Football League appearances in an eight-club career which spanned 30 years. Truly a giant of the game.

Viv Anderson's (extreme r) high boot fails to discourage Kenny Dalglish from nodding goalwards during Forest's City Ground League Cup semi-final clash with Liverpool.

ABOVE: The Scot, perhaps relieved to have escaped with his head intact, watches the flight of the ball optimistically …

ABOVE: … but Peter Shilton plunges acrobatically to his left to turn it round the post.

Charlie George's tenure at the City Ground was strictly of the temporary variety. The former Arsenal and Derby County star (left) made only four appearances for Forest during his stint on loan from Southampton early in 1980, but he did score the goal which beat Barcelona in this first leg of their European Super Cup encounter at the City Ground in January. That 1-0 victory was followed by a 1-1 draw at the Nou Camp a week later, so Brian Clough had another trophy in the cabinet.

ABOVE: Garry Birtles soars majestically above a Dynamo Berlin defender during Forest's 1-0 home defeat by the German club in the first leg of the European Cup quarter-final in March 1980. The Reds' hopes of retaining their trophy were written off by many pundits, but, inspired by the brilliance of two-goal Trevor Francis, they bounced back to win 3-1 in Germany to progress to the last four.

LEFT: The marauding Kenny Burns hassles the Dynamo rearguard, but the combative and vastly influential Scot collected a second booking which disqualified him for the difficult second leg. David Needham deputized, Forest progressed and Burns returned for the semi-final.

John Robertson nips ahead of fellow Scot Andy Gray to break up a Wolves attack during the 1980 League Cup final at Wembley. Gray had the last laugh, though, scoring the only goal of the game to take the trophy to Molineux.

Robbo is Rampant

Goal poacher Trevor Francis (number 10) turns away in glee after converting a John Robertson corner to put Forest in front after 33 minutes of their European Cup semi-final first leg against Ajax at the City Ground in April 1980. Martin O'Neill is looking for a team-mate to cuddle.

ABOVE: Garry Birtles – mobile, big-hearted and no mug with the ball at his feet – causes problems in the Ajax penalty box during the opening exchanges of the European Cup semi-final.

ABOVE: John Robertson, Forest's version of Merlin the Magician, slips away from his Ajax marker during the first leg.

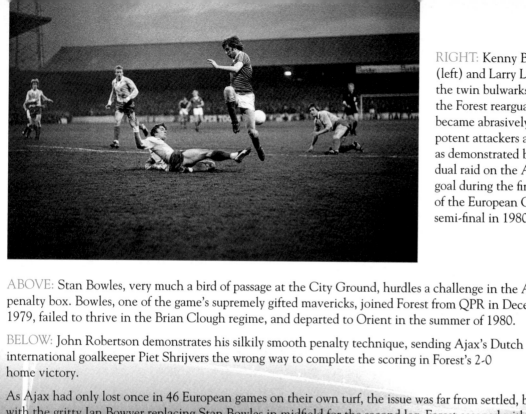

RIGHT: Kenny Burns (left) and Larry Lloyd, the twin bulwarks of the Forest rearguard, became abrasively potent attackers at need, as demonstrated by this dual raid on the Ajax goal during the first leg of the European Cup semi-final in 1980.

ABOVE: Stan Bowles, very much a bird of passage at the City Ground, hurdles a challenge in the Ajax penalty box. Bowles, one of the game's supremely gifted mavericks, joined Forest from QPR in December 1979, failed to thrive in the Brian Clough regime, and departed to Orient in the summer of 1980.

BELOW: John Robertson demonstrates his silkily smooth penalty technique, sending Ajax's Dutch international goalkeeper Piet Shrijvers the wrong way to complete the scoring in Forest's 2-0 home victory.

As Ajax had only lost once in 46 European games on their own turf, the issue was far from settled, but with the gritty Ian Bowyer replacing Stan Bowles in midfield for the second leg, Forest escaped with a single-goal defeat, thus winning 2-1 on aggregate to reach their second European Cup final on the trot.

CHAMPIONS OF EUROPE – AGAIN!

LEFT: Peter Shilton was by far the busier of the two goalkeepers in the 1980 European Cup final clash with Hamburg. Here he plucks yet another cross from the head of a German raider, watched by full-back Frank Gray.

The Promised Land. With his winner's medal in one fist, the handle of the European Cup in the other, Kenny Burns leads the celebrations after Hamburg have been vanquished.

LEFT: For the second successive season, John Robertson celebrates ecstatically after playing a crucial part in earning European Cup glory for Nottingham Forest. This time the affable Scottish international left-flank shuffler scored the only goal of the game to beat Hamburg, Kevin Keegan et al, in the Madrid final.

Robertson took possession near the left touchline, cut inside and played a one-two with Garry Birtles, then evaded a challenge just outside the box, strolled forward another pace and netted with a low right-footer which went in off the far post. The easy-going Robbo's reaction was a masterpiece of drollery: "Of course, I was very tired as well. It had been a long run by my standards!"

BELOW: Two great football men at the pinnacle of their profession. A beaming Peter Taylor and Brian Clough with the European Cup the day after Forest had retained the huge bauble by beating Hamburg in Madrid in 1980. Their achievement in transforming the hitherto unconsidered Midlands club into European champions, twice over, remains arguably the most colossal in the annals of the professional game.

LEFT: Forest skipper John McGovern atempts to wrong-foot fellow midfield dynamo, Willie Carr of Wolves, during the 1980 League Cup final at Wembley. Wolves won 1-0.

BELOW: John McGovern meets the Forest fans, brandishing the biggest bauble in club football, the European Cup, after the defeat of Hamburg in 1980.

FOOTBALL -STATS-

John McGovern

Name: John Prescott McGovern

Born: 1949

Playing Career: 1967–84

Clubs: Hartlepools United, Derby County, Leeds United, Nottingham Forest, Bolton Wanderers

Forest Appearances: 335

Goals: 11

Managerial Career: Bolton Wanderers, Rotherham United

–LEGENDS–

John McGovern

John McGovern was once described, memorably and aptly, as "the most extraordinary ordinary player" in England. In fact, he was ordinary only in the sense that he did not possess extravagant natural talent, while his industry and football intelligence as a central midfielder were exceptional. What made him truly extraordinary was his rise from the lower reaches of the professional game to lift the European Cup, not once but twice.

The opportunity to live this fantasy emanated from Brian Clough, who had managed the quiet, rather ungainly but endlessly efficient McGovern at Hartlepools United, Derby County and Leeds before making the whippet-slim Scottish under-23 international one of his first Forest signings in February 1975.

He went on to become captain, leading by example, and if idiots in the crowd sometimes barracked him when they were in need of a scapegoat and didn't want to slate one of their more fashionable favourites, then that didn't lessen his standing one jot with people who truly understood the game.

McGovern, who left to join Bolton in June 1982, goes down as an honest grafter with often-underrated vision, a man who made the absolute most of what ability he was born with. Clough employed him at four clubs, and his faith was repaid every time.

Perfectly balanced and with the ball seemingly glued to his boot, John Robertson attempts to slip away from Manchester United full-back Arthur Albiston at Old Trafford in January 1983. This time the Forest flankman's guile got him nowhere, however, as United prevailed 2-0.

–LEGENDS–

John Robertson

John Robertson was an unlikely-looking sporting hero, dumpy of build, pasty of face and with a distinct air of relaxation about him which did not suggest that athleticism, much less artistry, was on the agenda. Before the arrival of Brian Clough at the City Ground, he was overweight, scruffy, an inveterate smoker and seemingly destined for the soccer scrapheap. But Clough sensed an immense innate talent in the slovenly Scot, and duly transformed him into arguably the most enchanting wingman of his era.

Before long, thanks largely to his visionary boss but also to his own realization that he wasn't making the most of his glorious gifts, Robertson was making his erstwhile doubters look like idiots. There wasn't a player in the land who could create so much havoc in so little space. He rarely strayed from the left touchline, but even when apparently hemmed in with nowhere to go, he could shimmy and dart to wrong-foot his would-be markers, then use the half-yard of space thus created to deliver devilish away-swinging crosses into the path of his inrushing strikers.

Robertson set up the winning strike in the 1979 European Cup final for Trevor Francis, and showed his own predatory instinct by netting the only goal of the 1980 final. He was a one-off, a genuinely great player who might have slipped away from the game criminally unfulfilled, and that would have been a crying shame for all who celebrate the extraordinary in sport.

FOOTBALL –STATS–

John Robertson

Name: John Neilson Robertson

Born: 1953

Playing Career: 1970–86

Clubs: Nottingham Forest, Derby County

Forest Appearances: 514

Goals: 95

Scotland Appearances: 28

Goals: 8

ABOVE: Beaming match-winner John Robertson is right behind skipper John McGovern, who has the European Cup safely in his custody as Forest prepare to leave Madrid airport with their prize after beating Hamburg at the Bernabeu. Further up the steps are Kenny Burns and Peter Shilton.

–LEGENDS–

Brian Clough

Brian Clough was, without question, the most illustrious figure in Nottingham Forest history. He could be overbearing and rude, pompous and conceited, but he took the Reds by the collective scruff of the neck and guided them to pinnacles never even dreamed of by their most ardent supporters.

Having transformed Derby County but misfired at Leeds, Clough took over a nondescript Forest side floundering in the wrong half of the Second Division table in January 1975. Within 28 months he had led them into the top flight, a year later they were champions of England, one more season on they were Kings of Europe, and they went on to retain that crown in 1980. It was a unique and gargantuan achievement, the like of which had never been seen before and, in these days when money means more than ever in football, surely will never be seen again.

Together with his managerial partner, Peter Taylor, Clough recruited a series of unlikely characters while rehabilitating under-achievers already on the staff, none more dramatically than John Robertson, erstwhile a slow, overweight, under-motivated midfielder who soon became one of the most enchanting flankmen on the planet.

But Clough – who also listed four League Cup triumphs on his Forest record – wasn't infallible. As his reign moved on, he became increasingly eccentric, there were expensive buys which failed to reach expectations and there were times when his use of alcohol rendered him a parody of his former self.

It was overwhelmingly poignant that he presided over Forest's relegation in 1993, at the end of his final season at the City Ground, but even that could not wipe out the sheer splendour of what had gone before.

FOOTBALL –STATS–

Brian Clough

Name: Brian Howard Clough

Born: 1935

Died: 2004

Playing Career: 1952–64

Clubs: Middlesbrough, Sunderland

England Appearances: 2

Goals: 0

Managerial Career: Hartlepools United, Derby County, Brighton and Hove Albion, Leeds United, Nottingham Forest

Brian Clough on the Forest bench in 1988. Though there were still some triumphs to come, his best days were behind him.

Trevor Francis as Forest fans remember him best, wheeling away and saluting the crowd after scoring a goal, this time in the 3-1 victory over Sunderland at the City Ground in December 1980. The striker did not enjoy a long Nottingham sojourn – it lasted only from February 1979 to September 1981 – and it was marred by injuries, but his influence was profound.

The ball eludes Forest's flame-haired Scottish marksman Ian Wallace and Aston Villa centre-half Ken McNaught during the Midlanders' 2-2 draw at the City Ground in late December 1980. Villa finished the season as champions, while Forest dropped to seventh place in the table. Wallace cost £1.25 million from Coventry City and was a lively performer, but failed to live up to expectations.

Seasoned travellers: Peter Taylor and Brian Clough at the airport en route to Tokyo in February 1981 for Forest's World Club Championship clash with Nacional of Uruguay. The South Americans took an early lead which they never relinquished, despite Forest attacking for most of the match.

Forest stopper Kenny Burns and Liverpool striker Ian Rush chase a high ball at the City Ground in April 1981. The prolific Rush was a daunting opponent, but Burns' instinctive reading of the unfolding action enabled him to cope. The game finished 0-0.

Midfielder Mark Proctor shoots for goal, watched by his skipper John McGovern, during the 1-1 draw with Leeds United at Elland Road in March 1982. At this point Forest were going through a period of transition, and Proctor, a £425,000 recruit from Middlesbrough, was one of several major signings who didn't quite work out.

Period of Transition

Ouch! Forest centre-forward Justin Fashanu feels the full force of former Reds hero Kenny Burns' tackle in the springtime draw at Leeds. Fashanu, signed from Norwich City for £1 million during the previous summer, was a tortured soul who clashed repeatedly with Brian Clough and never settled at the City Ground, crossing the Trent to join Notts County in December 1982, having scored only three League goals for Forest.

Liverpool's Alan Hansen tussles for possession with Ian Wallace of Forest during the Merseysiders' 2-0 win at Anfield on May Day 1982. Ready to offer assistance is Mark Lawrenson, with whom Hansen formed arguably the finest central-defensive pairing of their generation.

159

Beating the Bhoys

Steve Hodge (right foreground) roars his delight after netting for the Reds during their UEFA Cup triumph over Celtic at Parkhead in December 1983 in front of nearly 67,000 fans, the biggest attendance at any Forest game to that point, Wembley appearances apart. The visitors prevailed 2-1 in this second leg – Colin Walsh was the other scorer – and on aggregate. Peter Davenport (left) is equally elated, a vivid contrast to the glum figure of Celtic full-back Danny McGrain.

ABOVE: A study in apprehension as Forest's defensive wall faces a free-kick from Celtic's Murdo MacLeod at Parkhead. The Reds' line consists of, left to right, Steve Wigley, Steve Hodge, Paul Hart, keeper Hans van Breukelen, Kenny Swain (behind MacLeod), Ian Bowyer, Garry Birtles and Peter Davenport.

ABOVE: Defenders Paul Hart (left) and Chris Fairclough (on ground) combine to deny Celtic raider Murdo MacLeod, who scored the Bhoys' lone reply to Forest's two strikes at Parkhead, which took them to the last eight of the UEFA Cup.

Peter Davenport, a quick and clever striker, unleashes a power drive during Forest's encouraging 2-0 home win over Anderlecht in the first leg of the UEFA Cup semi-final in April 1984. Alas, Steve Hodge's two goals were not enough to take the Reds to the final as they slumped to a controversial 3-0 second-leg reverse in Belgium. The shock turnaround featured several bizarre refereeing decisions which went against Forest, and later Anderlecht were fined and banned from Europe for bribing the official.

BELOW: Cultured sweeper cum midfield play-maker Johnny Metgod skirmishes for possession in Forest's 1-0 victory over Everton at the City Ground in the penultimate fixture of 1984/85. The Dutch international, a free-kick specialist signed from Real Madrid at the outset of the campaign, spent three seasons as a Red before joining Tottenham Hotspur for £250,000.

LEFT: "The Iron Man" and the silver salver. Nigel Clough receives the Young Player of the Month award from former Wolves manager Stan Cullis in February 1986. Cullis, renowned as a stern disciplinarian who expected his players to run through stone walls for him, was mightily impressed by the footballing development of the 19-year-old Clough, who was emerging as one of the most skilful and intelligent attackers in the land.

161

—LEGENDS— Ian Bowyer

There was little of the star about Ian Bowyer, but he was one of the key figures in the Clough regime which transformed Forest from perennial under-achievers into Kings of Europe. A supremely dedicated and versatile professional who could fill virtually any position at need, the Merseyside-born battler was brought to the City Ground from Orient by manager Dave Mackay in October 1973.

But it was not until Clough's arrival that Bowyer truly bloomed as a workaholic midfielder, topping the club's scoring chart with 16 senior goals in 1975–76. He played all but one game of the promotion campaign that followed, but then was ousted for part of the subsequent League title term owing to the signing of Archie Gemmill.

However, Bowyer proved impossible to discard, bouncing back in 1978–79, scoring the European Cup semi-final winner in Cologne, then featuring in consecutive final triumphs.

He was transferred to Sunderland in January 1981 as Clough began to reconstruct his squad, but he was welcomed back with open arms a year later, and soon became an inspirational captain, his experience invaluable to a young team.

When Bowyer was freed, at the age of 36, to join Hereford United in July 1987, he departed with the richly merited status of one of Forest's favourite sons.

Forest midfielder Ian Bowyer lunges, with typically courageous disregard for his own safety, in an unsuccessful attempt to block a shot from Chelsea's Ian Britton in the Stamford Bridge promotion battle of April 1977, in which the Londoners prevailed 2-1. In the end both clubs went up, Chelsea in second place behind champions Wolves, and Forest in third, three points further adrift.

FOOTBALL —STATS—

Ian Bowyer

Name: Ian Bowyer

Born: 1951

Playing Career: 1968–90

Clubs: Manchester City, Orient, Nottingham Forest, Sunderland, Hereford United

Forest Appearances: 562

Goals: 97

Managerial Career: Hereford United

–LEGENDS– Neil Webb

As a sweet-passing midfield general, Neil Webb was easy on the eye. At his best he roved artistically, his vision, accuracy and composure reeking of class. He packed a rasping shot, too, which ensured he delivered his share of goals.

But Webb was something of an enigma. When the Muse was not with him he tended to drift frustratingly on the fringe of the action, his deceptively languid style – he wasn't lazy, it was just the awkward way he ran – irritating some supporters, who reckoned he lacked urgency.

After emulating his father, Doug, by making his senior debut for Reading, his home-town club, Webb shone for Portsmouth, whom Brian Clough paid £250,000 for his services in June 1985, beating off competition from several other suitors. He settled rapidly at the City Ground, dovetailing fluently with Nigel Clough as the creative centre of an entertaining side.

Inevitably, Webb became a target of richer clubs, and in June 1989 Alex Ferguson concluded a protracted quest by signing him for £1.5 million. Sadly for the midfielder, he soon suffered a severe Achilles injury and was never quite the same again. He did set up the FA Cup winner for Lee Martin in 1990, but he never truly recaptured his former momentum and was sold back to Forest for £800,000 in November 1992. Alas, fitness and form proved elusive and he made his final senior move, to Grimsby Town, in 1996.

Manchester United's Paul McGrath can't prevent Neil Webb from shooting at goal during the FA Cup quarter-final at Old Trafford in March 1989. Forest won 1-0.

FOOTBALL –STATS–

Neil Webb

Name: Neil John Webb

Born: 1963

Playing Career: 1980–96

Clubs: Reading, Portsmouth, Nottingham Forest, Manchester United, Swindon Town on loan, Grimsby Town

Forest Appearances: 222

Goals: 59

England Appearances: 26

Goals: 4

Knocking Out United

Manchester United's Gordon Strachan is dispossessed by a trademark sliding tackle from Stuart Pearce during Forest's rousing FA Cup quarter-final victory at Old Trafford in March 1989. Steve Hodge (right) might be wincing at the ferocious power of his team-mate's challenge, while United's Mal Donaghy can be grateful he's not on the receiving end.

ABOVE: Midfielder Garry Parker turns away in triumph after side-footing the only goal of Forest's FA Cup triumph in Manchester following some scintillating wing play by Franz Carr. The appalled United defenders are, left to right, Mal Donaghy, Paul McGrath, Steve Bruce and Lee Sharpe.

BELOW: Forest full-back Brian Laws takes to the air in spectacular fashion to deny Manchester United winger Ralph Milne during the FA Cup encounter. The much-travelled Laws, who served seven clubs during his career, was a solid performer who earned England "B" and Football League call-ups.

League Cup Number Three

LEFT: Just three weeks short of 30 years since the clubs had last met at Wembley, in the FA Cup final of 1959, Nottingham Forest and Luton Town take to the Wembley turf to play for the League Cup in April 1989. Brian Clough, impeccably turned out in club blazer and slacks, heads the Forest column, while Ray Harford is in charge of the Hatters.

ABOVE: A Forest contingent on a well-earned Wembley lap of honour after beating Luton Town 3-1 in the final of the League Cup. Nigel Clough (right) who contributed two goals, including one from the penalty spot, leads the way. Striding out alongside him are, left to right, Des Walker, Stuart Pearce and Brian Laws. Forest's other goal came from Neil Webb.

Catastrophe at Hillsborough

LEFT: Stuart Pearce and two Liverpool opponents in the opening minutes of the FA Cup semi-final at Hillsborough, utterly oblivious of the sickening events which were already beginning to unfold.

The encounter on 15th April 1989 descended into an afternoon of stark tragedy that would leave an indelible scar on English football. Ninety-six fans lost their lives as the result of a horrendous terrace crush, the full extent of which began to unfold soon after the match kicked off. The semi-final, utterly irrelevant in the traumatic circumstances, was swiftly abandoned by referee Ray Lewis (below left), and instead of snapping scenes of football action, photographers trained their cameras on police and officials striving to bring order to the hellish scene (below).

As football attempts to return to something approaching normality in the immediate wake of the Hillsborough calamity, Forest and Liverpool captains Stuart Pearce and Ronnie Whelan lead their teams out at Old Trafford for the reconvened FA Cup semi-final.

The players of Liverpool and Nottingham Forest line up at Old Trafford for an FA Cup semi-final like no other. To call the atmosphere sombre would be a colossal understatement, and it was remarkable that they were able to put on such a competitive contest in the wake of the disaster.

BELOW: England team-mates John Barnes of Liverpool and Forest's Des Walker face each other at Old Trafford after the FA decided that the show must go on. Liverpool won comfortably by three goals to Forest's one, which was scored by Neil Webb.

BELOW: Forest spearhead Lee Chapman attempts to escape the close attention of Steve McMahon during the FA Cup semi-final. Some believed the extensively travelled Chapman had seen his best days when he joined Forest from the French club, Niort, at the start of the season, but he went on to play a major part in Leeds United's title success in 1991–92.

-LEGENDS-

Nigel Clough

Nigel Clough was a footballer for the connoisseur. He never had to rely on the power and pace, the sheer athleticism, that dominates the modern game. Rather he majored on delicacy of touch, subtlety of pass and intelligence of run to make him one of the most attractive, and successful, makers and takers of goals in Nottingham Forest's modern history.

Certainly any daft accusations of nepotism, Nigel being the son of manager Brian, were soon scotched after Clough Jnr was recruited from non-League Heanor Town as a richly promising 18-year-old in September 1984.

His subsequently well-documented lack of pace was always evident, but he rendered that irrelevant by the speed and perception of his thinking, which enabled him to observe the old adage of "making the ball do the work". Not only did he shine himself, but as the team's attacking fulcrum Nigel helped to bring the best out of such colleagues as Lee Chapman, Nigel Jemson and Teddy Sheringham.

A player of his flair and dexterity appeared to be made for Liverpool, to whom he was sold for £2.275 million in the summer of 1993, but after a scintillating start he faded during a troubled period for the Anfield club, failing to realize his vast potential.

A brief loan stint back at the City Ground in 1996–97 brought no reversal of fortune, and Clough turned his thoughts to management.

FOOTBALL -STATS-

Nigel Clough

Name: Nigel Howard Clough

Born: 1966

Playing Career: 1984–97

Clubs: Nottingham Forest, Liverpool, Manchester City, Sheffield Wednesday

Forest Appearances: 398

Goals: 130

England Appearances: 14

Goals: 0

Managerial Career: Burton Albion, Derby County

ABOVE: Fourteen-year-old Nigel Clough and his two footballing mentors.

LEFT: An exuberant Nigel Clough leaps skywards to salute Toddi Orlygsson's goal in the 1-1 draw with Chelsea at the City Ground in February 1990.

OPPOSITE INSET: Nigel Clough bursts between two Spurs defenders, Mauricio Taricco (left) and David Howells, during the second leg of the League Cup semi-final at White Hart Lane in March 1992. Clough wasn't renowned for his pace, but he more than made up for that with his craft.

OPPOSITE: Stuart Pearce can only spectate helplessly as Mark Robins nods the goal which evicted Forest from the FA Cup in January 1990, and which is popularly believed to have saved the job of Old Trafford boss Alex Ferguson. That is always denied by Manchester United insiders, but the fact remains that the future knight would have faced an immensely difficult springtime had his underdogs – struggling desperately in the League at the time – not upset the odds at the City Ground.

BELOW: Forest full-back Brian Laws (right) mops up as Manchester United attackers Mark Hughes (left) and eventual match-winner Mark Robins threaten mayhem in their FA Cup clash at the City Ground. Des Walker is the other defender.

That Same Old Feeling

ABOVE: Striker Nigel Jemson scores the only goal of the 1990 League Cup final at Wembley, knocking in the rebound after Oldham Athletic goalkeeper Andy Rhodes had blocked his first effort. The decisive strike came early in the second half after delightful approach work by Nigel Clough.

RIGHT: They didn't even dream it at the time, but when Forest players faced the cameras with the League Cup after defeating Oldham, they were celebrating – with all due respect to the Zenith Data Systems Cup triumph of 1992 – the last major trophy of Brian Clough's career.

–LEGENDS–

Des Walker

Searing pace was the bedrock of Des Walker's game, but there was rather more to the Forest and England central defender than the ability to outsprint virtually any striker with whom he was faced.

The unassuming, undemonstrative Londoner – he was rejected by Spurs as a boy – was also renowned for his unflappability, no matter how frenetically the action raged around him. He was a brisk tackler, too, adept at timing his challenges perfectly even at top speed, and he was terrific in the air. Then there was his reading of the game, which enabled him to make countless interceptions, often snuffing out attacks in the early stages of menace rather than at the last ditch.

What Walker wasn't – and nobody is perfect – was a brilliant distributor of the ball, so invariably he was sensible enough to lay off safe, simple passes as soon as he had won possession, which enabled the team's natural creators, of which there were always plenty among the City Ground ranks, to take up the attacking baton.

Walker, who at his peak was coveted by many of Europe's top clubs, especially following his exceptional form in the 1990 World Cup finals, served Forest in two spells, from 1983–84 to 1991–92 – after which he was sold to Sampdoria for £1.5 million – and as a veteran from 2002–03 to 2004–05.

Des Walker climbs above Manchester United's Mark Hughes (centre) and Brian McClair as Forest knock Alex Ferguson's team out of the FA Cup at Old Trafford in March 1989. The London-born centre-half became a key man for Forest in the mid-1980s and continued to improve as the decade wore on.

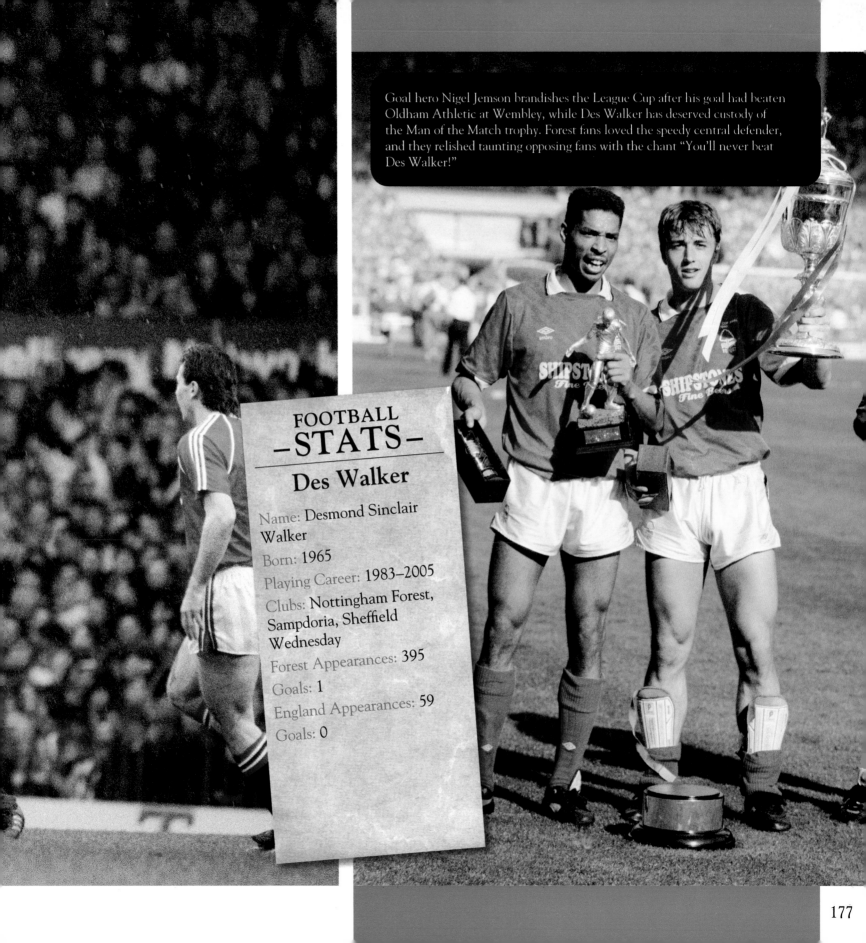

Goal hero Nigel Jemson brandishes the League Cup after his goal had beaten Oldham Athletic at Wembley, while Des Walker has deserved custody of the Man of the Match trophy. Forest fans loved the speedy central defender, and they relished taunting opposing fans with the chant "You'll never beat Des Walker!"

FOOTBALL
-STATS-

Des Walker

Name: Desmond Sinclair Walker

Born: 1965

Playing Career: 1983–2005

Clubs: Nottingham Forest, Sampdoria, Sheffield Wednesday

Forest Appearances: 395

Goals: 1

England Appearances: 59

Goals: 0

Force of Nature

A new force of nature at the Forest. Irishman Roy Keane, who would become one of the best footballers in the world as a Manchester United man, shoots for goal during the 4-0 FA Cup semi-final drubbing of West Ham United at Villa Park in April 1991.

In the mood and well-nigh impossible to stop, Paul Gascoigne takes on Garry Parker (left), having already left a gaggle of would-be markers in his wake during Forest's 1-1 draw at White Hart Lane in May 1991. When the teams met again, two weeks later in the FA Cup final, the Tottenham star was not quite so fluent …

"Psycho" is on his way to Wembley and he's savouring the moment. Stuart Pearce, who netted with his unfavoured right foot in the Villa Park win over West Ham, looks forward to his first appearance in an FA Cup final in 1991.

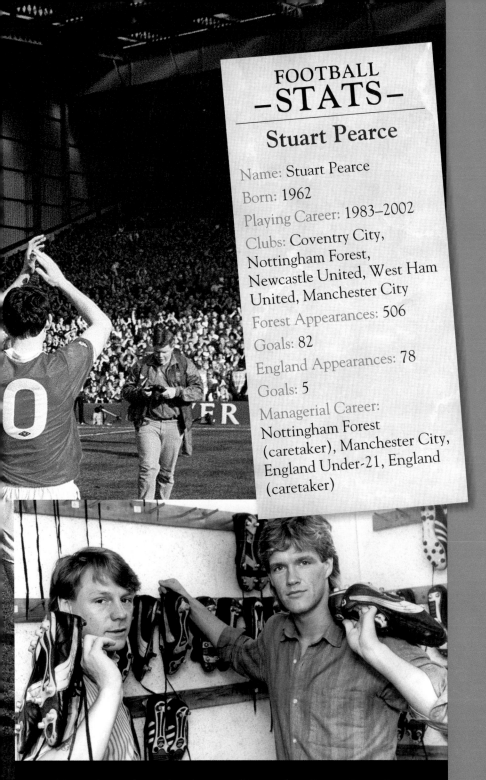

FOOTBALL –STATS–

Stuart Pearce

Name: Stuart Pearce

Born: 1962

Playing Career: 1983–2002

Clubs: Coventry City, Nottingham Forest, Newcastle United, West Ham United, Manchester City

Forest Appearances: 506

Goals: 82

England Appearances: 78

Goals: 5

Managerial Career: Nottingham Forest (caretaker), Manchester City, England Under-21, England (caretaker)

A red-letter day in the modern history of Nottingham Forest. Stuart Pearce (left) and Ian Butterworth collect their boots from the Coventry City training ground after agreeing to join Nottingham Forest in a £450,000 package deal in May 1985. After 15 months and 33 games, central defender Butterworth had moved on to Norwich City, but left-back Pearce – or "Psycho", to use the affectionate tag bestowed on him in time – was set to become one of the most revered performers the City Ground would ever know.

–LEGENDS–

Stuart Pearce

During his dozen years as Forest left-back, from 1985 to 1997, Stuart Pearce's snarling aggression for club and country – he remains the Reds' most-capped player, having made 76 of his 78 England appearances during his City Ground tenure – rendered him a national institution.

Pearce was a natural defender, with all the courage and technical expertise that entails, but he was also a formidable, even intimidating, operator when surging forward into attack, his buccaneering forays frequently climaxing with an explosive left-foot shot.

His appeal as folk hero was widened still further by his "everyman" image. Pearce was a late starter in the game, having worked as an electrician and not leaving non-League Wealdstone for Coventry City until he was 21 in October 1983. Some 20 months later he had been recruited to Forest by Brian Clough at a cost of £240,000 and, after a slightly slow start, within two years he was skipper.

For all his comic-book image as "Psycho", he was notably level-headed, a much-needed tough nut in a team that played attractive football; and the fans loved him unconditionally.

When Frank Clark departed as manager with Forest bottom of the Premier League table in December 1996, Pearce became player-caretaker boss until the appointment of Dave Bassett in March. In the following summer, aged 35 and having just experienced the trauma of relegation, he left the City Ground to join Newcastle United.

One That Got Away

LEFT: A two-handed greeting for Princess Diana from Brian Clough ahead of the 1991 FA Cup final at Wembley. Brian Laws (left) and Stuart Pearce look suitably gratified by the proximity of royalty – and they are impressed by the princess, too …

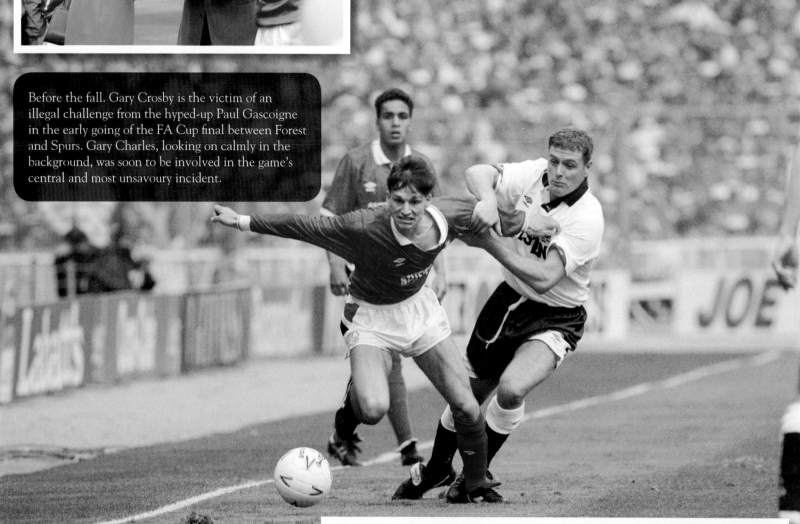

Before the fall. Gary Crosby is the victim of an illegal challenge from the hyped-up Paul Gascoigne in the early going of the FA Cup final between Forest and Spurs. Gary Charles, looking on calmly in the background, was soon to be involved in the game's central and most unsavoury incident.

RIGHT: What might have been the decisive moment of the final turned out to be nothing of the sort. Having perpetrated the wildest of challenges on poor Gary Charles, the stricken Paul Gascoigne signals for help. Gazza's self-inflicted agony put him out of the match, and out of the game for a year. Stuart Pearce scored from the free-kick following this incident in the 15th minute, but Spurs fought back to win 2-1.

ABOVE: Stuart Pearce (centre) has just got Forest off to a glorious start by netting with a trademark free-kick following Paul Gascoigne's madcap tackle on Gary Charles. Sadly for the Reds, this was their only celebration of an ultimately disappointing afternoon, which was to turn particularly desperate for Des Walker (second left). The England central defender was responsible for the own goal in extra time which decided the destination of the trophy.

ABOVE: "I say, you fellows. This is how I see it …" Forest skipper Stuart Pearce issues instructions during the FA Cup final defeat by Spurs.

It was only the Zenith Data Systems Cup final, but Wembley victories are always welcome. Here Kingsley Black fires home one of Forest's goals in the 3-2 win over Southampton in March 1992. Scot Gemmill, who contributed a brace, was the Reds' other scorer.

Revenge is Sweet

ABOVE: England team-mates Des Walker of Forest and Tottenham's Gary Lineker tussle for possession at White Hart Lane in the second leg of their League Cup semi-final meeting in March 1992. Forest won 2-1 to make up, at least in part, for their FA Cup final defeat by Spurs some 10 months earlier.

ABOVE: Forest striker Teddy Sheringham squirms away from a typically robust challenge from Spurs defender Pat van den Hauwe during the second leg of the League Cup semi-final at White Hart Lane in March 1992. Sheringham was a thinking man's striker, not blessed with pace but technically accomplished and intelligent. His career blossomed following his transfer to Tottenham Hotspur in August 1992 and subsequently peaked with Manchester United.

A Dismal Day

High-kicking Paul Ince looks to be favourite in this challenge with Forest's Kingsley Black (left) and Scot Gemmill during the 1992 League Cup final. The game, which Manchester United won 1-0, was a poor one, wth Brian Clough's men barely threatening their opponents' goal.

Scot Gemmill, son of former Forest favourite Archie, is the man in possession during the final, though Brian McClair (right) is about to challenge, and Paul Ince is on his tail.

Role reversal. Manchester United's precocious young star Ryan Giggs makes the tackle, while Forest defender Des Walker attempts to dance away from the challenge.

–LEGENDS–

Roy Keane

Anybody with half an eye who watched Forest straining gamely enough, but without sufficient collective quality or conviction, against relegation from the Premier League in 1992–93, realized very quickly that within their largely threadbare ranks was one young man who might have it in him to reach the stars.

That was midfielder Roy Keane, signed for £20,000 from the Irish club Cobh Ramblers as an 18-year-old in June 1990 and promoted almost immediately to the status of first-team regular. Clearly a ferociously driven individual, desperate to win every challenge, every game, as he charged from box to box on missions both creative and destructive, he stood out like a diamond in a box of toffees.

Though he was immensely raw, the quality of his passing and tackling, the instinctive sharpness of his positional play, and his overweening hunger for victory marked him out for greatness, and so it proved.

In the summer of 1993, as a Brian Clough-less Forest contemplated life in the second tier, Kenny Dalglish of Blackburn Rovers believed he had secured Keane's services, only to be beaten to the deal by Alex Ferguson, who paid a British record £3.75 million to add the fiery youngster to his newly crowned League champions at Old Trafford.

That he tasted success with Manchester United was entirely predictable, but Roy Keane went beyond that, maturing – if that is the right word in his case – into arguably the most influential player in the land for the next decade. What might Forest have achieved had he remained in Nottingham? It doesn't even bear thinking about.

FOOTBALL
–STATS–

Roy Keane

Name: Roy Maurice Keane

Born: 1971

Playing Career: 1990–2006

Clubs: Nottingham Forest, Manchester United, Celtic

Forest Appearances: 149

Goals: 31

Republic of Ireland Appearances: 67

Goals: 9

Managerial Career: Sunderland, Ipswich Town

ABOVE: Roy Keane in typically combative mode, mixing it with Spurs' Paul Stewart in the League Cup semi-final second leg at White Hart Lane in March 1992.

LEFT: Roy Keane attempts to sway past Steve Bruce during the 1992 League Cup final. A little more than a year later, the pugnacious Irishman was destined to become a comrade-in-arms of the Manchester United skipper at Old Trafford.

Hope Springs Eternal

Hope springs eternal. Brian Clough salutes the Forest fans with an optimistic thumbs-up in August 1992. Sadly, it was a season which was to end in disillusionment, relegation and the retirement of the club's greatest ever manager.

Getting close to a poignant farewell: a solemn Brian Clough, his team fighting unavailingly against relegation, looks ready for the worst in February 1993.

GOODBYE CLOUGHIE

Fans pay tribute on Forest's tearful day

By DAVID MOORE

One of the most talented and intelligent footballers Forest have ever produced, Nigel Clough takes a breather during England's tour of the United States in the summer of 1993.

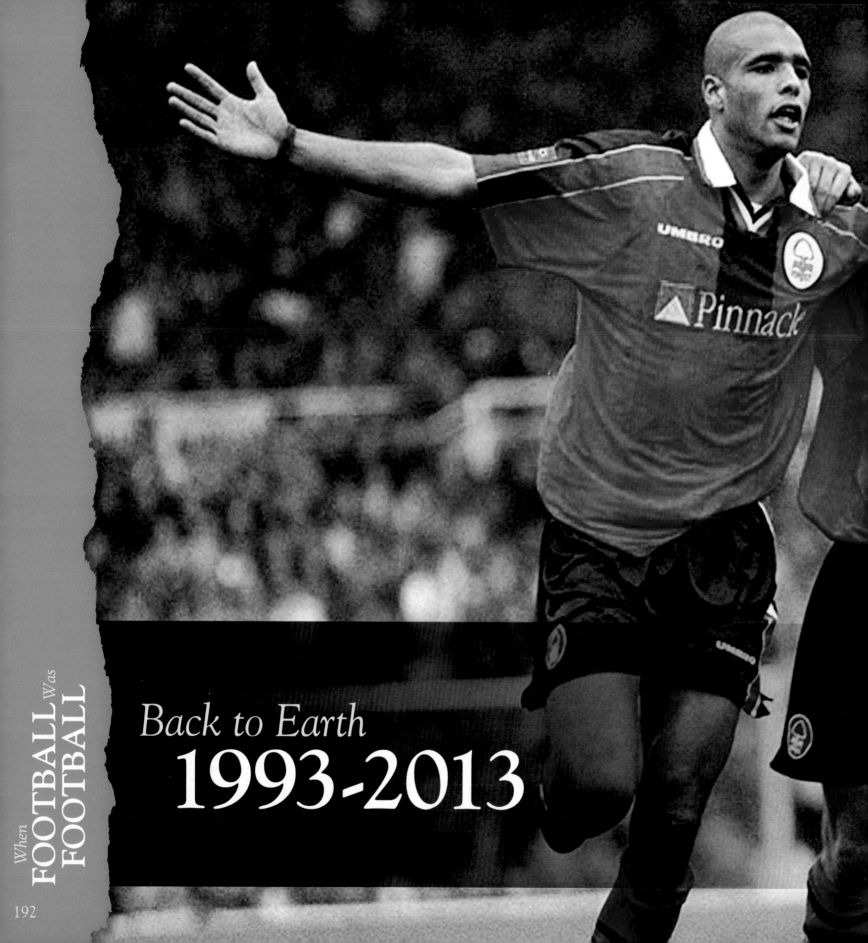

Back to Earth
1993-2013

Another game, another goal celebration for the prolific Pierre van Hooijdonk (left) during Nottingham Forest's exhilarating progress to the First Division crown in 1997–98. This time the eccentric but notably prolific Dutchman has netted in the 2-1 triumph over Birmingham City at St Andrew's in March, and is joined in his revels by Steve Stone (centre) and Kevin Campbell, with Thierry Bonalair behind.

1993 Frank Clark takes the Forest hot seat. 1994 Forest promoted as Second Division runners-up to Crystal Palace. 1995 Clark guides Forest to third place in Premiership. 1996 Clark departs, replaced by Stuart Pearce. 1997 Forest go down as bottom club, Dave Bassett steps up from general manager's role to take charge of team. 1998 Promoted as champions under Dave Bassett. 1999 Demoted again, this time under Ron Atkinson; David Platt takes the reins. 2001 Platt goes, Paul Hart is the new gaffer. 2004 Hart out, Joe Kinnear in, relegation averted, Joe Kinnear resigns. 2005 Gary Megson is the new manager; relegated to third tier. 2006 Colin Calderwood replaces Megson after caretakers Frank Barlow and Ian McParland have avoided another demotion and just missed play-off place. 2008 Promoted to second flight, Calderwood sacked in December. 2009 Billy Davies takes control of the team. 2010 Lost in play-offs. 2011 Another play-offs defeat. Steve McClaren gets the hot seat, then Steve Cotterill. 2012 Owner and ex-chairman Nigel Doughty dies; Al-Hasawi family of Kuwait takes control; Cotterill departs. 2013 Alex McLeish is Forest boss for 40 days, Billy Davies returns in February.

After the Gold Rush

The men who followed Brian Clough were always going to be on a hiding to nothing. Nobody could hope to compare favourably to the great man, but some of his successors didn't do at all badly, notably Frank Clark and Dave Bassett, Colin Calderwood for a while and Billy Davies, now in his second City Ground tenure.

Of course, expectations had to be lowered in the wake of the best manager England never had, a man with a truly golden gift for getting the best out of a football club. But there have been three promotions to savour and some thoroughbred footballers to enjoy, notably Stan Collymore and Pierre van Hooijdonk, though it must be admitted that this pair of extravagantly gifted goal-getters did have their little eccentricities!

The important thing is that, under ambitious new owners, Nottingham Forest will go on – and after nearly a century and a half of colourful history, anything else would be unthinkable.

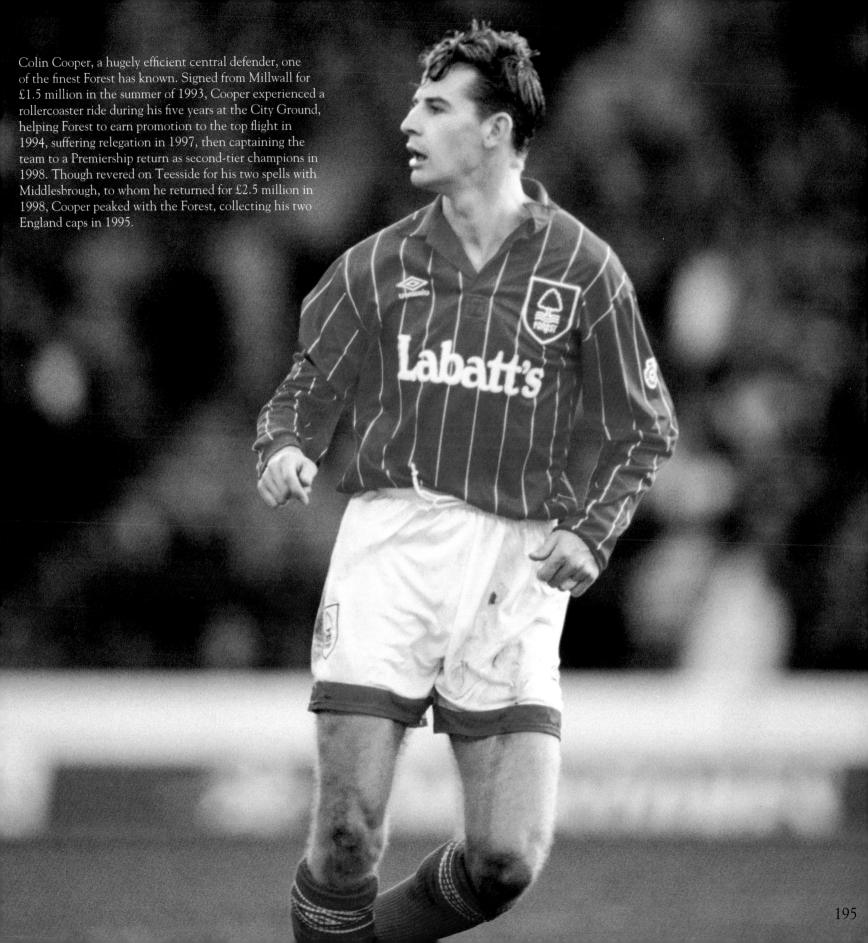

Colin Cooper, a hugely efficient central defender, one of the finest Forest has known. Signed from Millwall for £1.5 million in the summer of 1993, Cooper experienced a rollercoaster ride during his five years at the City Ground, helping Forest to earn promotion to the top flight in 1994, suffering relegation in 1997, then captaining the team to a Premiership return as second-tier champions in 1998. Though revered on Teesside for his two spells with Middlesbrough, to whom he returned for £2.5 million in 1998, Cooper peaked with the Forest, collecting his two England caps in 1995.

Gone But
Not Forgotten

Brian Clough at the launch of his autobiography in 1994. As Michael Parkinson said on the back cover: "Someone should stick a preservation order on him before it's too late – the manager is a national treasure."

Manager of the Month

Frank Clark, who replaced Brian Clough as manager of Nottingham Forest in 1993 and led them back to the Premiership at the first time of asking as First Division runners-up to Crystal Palace. Clark, a stalwart full-back in Forest's first European Cup-winning side, then exceeded most expectations by guiding his team to third place in the top tier in 1995. Here he brandishes a Manager of the Month award in the autumn of 1995, ironically only a few days after a 7-0 thrashing at Blackburn. Thereafter, the fortunes of both Forest and Frank took a turn for the worse, and he resigned midway through the 1996–97 campaign with his relegation-doomed side at the bottom of the table.

198

ABOVE: Goalkeeper Mark Crossley hams it up for the cameras at the City Ground in November 1995. The big Yorkshireman was ever-present in Forest's 56-match campaign, with the highlight being his three saves in the FA Cup penalty shoot-out victory over Spurs which saw them through to the quarter-finals. Crossley went on to make more than 300 appearances for the club before moving to Middlesbrough in 2000.

RIGHT: Striker Bryan Roy, signed by Forest for nearly £3 million from the Italian club Foggia in the summer of 1994, fresh from shining for Holland during the 1994 World Cup finals in the USA. The Dutchman meshed instantly with Stan Collymore, the pair scoring 40 goals between them in all competitions as the newly promoted Reds finished third in the Premiership in what proved to be their only season together. Without the departed Collymore in the two subsequent terms, Roy was never quite the same force, though he did help the Reds to reach the quarter-finals of the UEFA Cup in 1995–96. Knee trouble reduced his effectiveness, and in 1997 he was sold to Hertha Berlin for £1.5 million.

"Psycho's" Sombre Exit

Stuart Pearce announces his resignation as player-caretaker boss of Nottingham Forest in the troubled spring of 1997, during which the cash-strapped club had been engulfed in uncertainty about rival takeover bids. "Psycho" stepped courageously into the void left by Frank Clark in December, inheriting a side at rock bottom, and hinting at a miracle when he guided them to five successive victories in January.

As a result he picked up the Manager of the Month award, but even the indefatigable Forest hero found the odds still facing him to be insurmountable. The Reds could muster only one more win during the rest of the campaign and finished bottom of the pile, leaving Pearce to make a sombre exit. The old warrior was far from finished, though, continuing his playing career with Newcastle, West Ham and Manchester City, and not laying aside his boots until he was 40.

On the Up

If you want to win promotion, Dave Bassett's your man! When he led Forest back to the top flight at the first attempt in 1997–98, it was the seventh time he had taken a side up a division, a Football League record.

Bassett had been the club's general manager since February 1997, then took over responsibility for the team when Stuart Pearce resigned in the May. The new boss was, and remains, one of the most knowledgeable men in the game, a brilliant organizer and a defensive specialist, but also capable of extracting the best from his front men, in this case Pierre van Hooijdonk and the sometimes underrated former Arsenal star Kevin Campbell.

–LEGENDS–

Pierre van Hooijdonk

Having spent two seasons in the company of Stan Collymore, Forest knew all about dealing with brilliant but eccentric strikers, and they found another in Pierre van Hooijdonk.

The lanky Dutchman was signed from Celtic for £4.5 million in March 1997 in the wake of an acrimonious wage dispute at Parkhead, and he made an unremarkable start at the City Ground. That spring Forest were fighting to preserve their top-flight status, and the newcomer couldn't prevent relegation. However, in 1997–98 he was a revelation, forming a potent dual spearhead with Kevin Campbell and plundering 34 goals – 29 of them in the League, more than anyone else in the land that term – as Dave Bassett's side lifted the First Division title.

Usually operating slightly behind the former Arsenal man, van Hooijdonk was quick and strong, effective in the air and on the ground, and menacingly unpredictable. Certainly goalkeepers struggled to follow the flight-path of his trademark long-distance free-kicks, which swerved so unnervingly that eight of them found the net during the campaign.

Sadly it was all too good to last. That summer he asked for a move, citing Forest's failure to strengthen the squad and questioning their ambition. When the request was turned down he went on strike until early November before swallowing his pride and returning to a team mired at the foot of the table. Van Hooijdonk's comeback made little difference: Forest went down and at season's end he was sold to Vitesse Arnhem.

Forest strikeforce Pierre van Hooijdonk (left) and Kevin Campbell celebrate a successful penalty kick by the giant Dutchman during the 3-2 victory over second-tier strugglers Manchester City at Maine Road in December 1997. Van Hooijdonk struck twice from the spot, with Campbell contributing the other goal.

FOOTBALL –STATS–

Pierre van Hooijdonk

Name: Petrus Ferdinandus Johannes van Hooijdonk

Born: 1969

Playing Career: 1989–2007

Clubs: RBC Roosendaal, NAC Breda, Celtic, Nottingham Forest, Vitesse Arnhem, Benfica, Feyenoord, Fenerbahce

Forest Appearances: 77

Goals: 41

Holland Appearances: 46

Goals: 14

–LEGENDS– Stan Collymore

Fabulous though his goals-to-games ratio was during his all-too-brief City Ground sojourn – 44 hits in 76 outings is remarkable at any level – Nottingham Forest never witnessed the full flowering of the wondrous talent that was Stan Collymore. But then, neither did anybody else.

During his two terms in Nottingham, the big, rangy Midlander was the star attraction as Forest won promotion to the top tier in 1993–94, then finished third in the Premiership at the first attempt. His best-loved manoeuvre was to pick up the ball deep inside his own half, then carry it past a steady stream of opponents before hitting the net with a spectacular drive. His ball control and vision were the equal of any play-maker, he thrashed home goals from every angle, he could run forever and he was a swashbuckling entertainer – so what prevented Collymore from hitting the game's giddiest heights?

Well, for all that he was an eloquent, intelligent and sensitive fellow, there were serious downsides to his character. He could be sulky, he could be egotistical and some of his off-the-field antics were self-destructive. He fell out with many of his Forest team-mates, who eventually refused to join in his goal celebrations, and it was hardly a surprise when the man whom manager Frank Clark had bought for £2.5 million from Southend United in July 1993 was sold to Liverpool for £8.5 million only two years later.

Stan Collymore had the raw ability to become the best footballer in the country, but he fell short, at Anfield and at his four subsequent clubs. If only …

RIGHT: The enigmatic Stan Collymore, arguably the most naturally gifted footballer in Nottingham Forest history.

FOOTBALL –STATS–
Stan Collymore

Name: Stanley Victor Collymore
Born: 1971
Playing Career: 1989–2001
Clubs: Crystal Palace, Southend United, Nottingham Forest, Liverpool, Aston Villa, Fulham, Leicester City, Bradford City
Forest Appearances: 76
Goals: 44
England Appearances: 3
Goals: 0

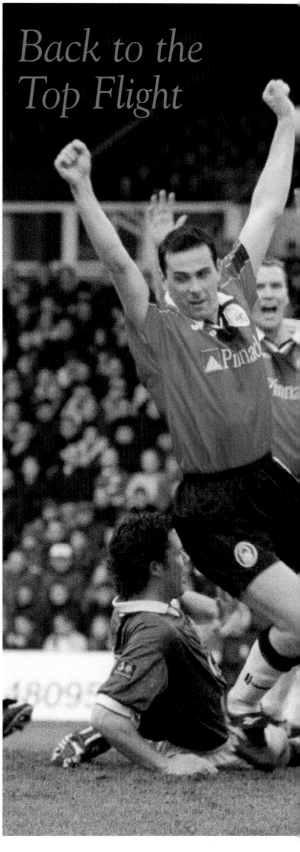

ABOVE: Forest's England international midfielder Geoff Thomas has his eyes glued to the ball during the Reds' 1-0 win at Portsmouth in February 1998, on the way to the Division One championship.

After his retirement as a player in 2002, the much-travelled Mancunian overcame leukaemia and has since set up the Geoff Thomas Foundation to battle blood cancer.

RIGHT: Forest centre-half Steve Chettle hails his only goal of the 1997–98 Division One title campaign, the winner against Portsmouth at Fratton Park. Nottingham boy Chettle made some 500 senior appearances for his local club before leaving for Barnsley in November 1999. A commendably consistent performer who earned a dozen England under-21 caps, he made his Reds debut during 1987–88 and went on to become one of the club's most loyal servants.

Steve Stone, a midfield dynamo who combined industry, endurance and quality on the ball, and but for injuries would surely have collected more than his nine England caps. Still, the deeply committed Northeasterner proved a key man for Forest throughout the 1990s before moving to Aston Villa for £5.5 million at the end of the decade.

Destined for Great Things

ABOVE: Richly promising young Nottingham Forest centre-half Michael Dawson beats Wolves' Kenny Miller to the ball during a 2-1 defeat at Molineux in November 2004. Though his progress with Forest had been disrupted by injuries, Dawson was clearly rich in potential, having already been made Forest skipper and earned England under-21 honours. Thus with the Reds toiling in the second tier, it came as no surprise when the tall, slim Yorkshireman joined Spurs in January 2005 in an £8 million package deal which included Forest team-mate Andy Reid.

RIGHT: The rain lashes down at the City Ground as Forest's David Johnson attempts to escape the close attentions of Joleon Lescott, the Wolves central defender, in October 2004. Forest won 1-0, courtesy of a strike by Andy Reid, but it was only their second League victory of a dire campaign, at the end of which they were demoted to the third tier. Gary Megson replaced Joe Kinnear as manager in mid-season, but couldn't stop the rot.

When the Going Gets Tough ...

LEFT: Big Kelvin Wilson towers over Birmingham City's Marcus Bent as the Forest defender clears his lines in the 1-1 draw at the City Ground in November 2008. Having won promotion back to the second flight during the previous spring, the Reds found the going tough, finishing 19th in the division, uncomfortably adjacent to the relegation zone. Boss Colin Calderwood was sacked in December, having presided over only four League victories, and was succeeded by Billy Davies.

ABOVE: Welsh international full-back Chris Gunter (right), here jousting with Birmingham City's Keith Fahey in a goalless FA Cup stalemate at the City Ground in January 2010, was one of the stars of an impressive but ultimately unfortunate term for Billy Davies' Reds. They finished third in the second flight – albeit a dozen points adrift of second-placed West Bromwich Albion and no fewer than 23 behind champions Newcastle United – but lost in the play-offs to sixth-placed Blackpool, who had garnered nine fewer points over the season.

BELOW: Robbie Earnshaw, here being comprehensively outjumped by Wolves' Christophe Berra, was nevertheless one of the main reasons Forest avoided the drop in 2008–09. In his first season at the City Ground following his £2.65 million move from local rivals Derby County, the perky Welsh international striker was the club's top scorer with a dozen League goals, plus five more in the knockout competitions.

LEFT: Burly Forest stopper Wes Morgan is all over Wolves' Sylvan Ebanks-Blake in the all-Midlands clash at the City Ground in March 2009 in which Billy Davies' team were fighting to stay in the second tier. They lost this battle 1-0 but won the war, finishing seven points clear of demoted Norwich City.

Home is the Hero

More than a decade had passed since Andy Reid (right) made his Forest entrance as a subtly gifted, left-sided midfielder, but when the popular Republic of Ireland international returned to the City Ground in 2011 – having put in stints with Spurs, Charlton, Sunderland, Sheffield United and Blackpool – all the old artistry and grace were intact. Here he comes over all balletic when confronted by West Bromwich Albion's Youssef Mulumbu in a pre-season friendly at the City Ground in August 2012.

Acknowledgements

To Mirrorpix maestros David Scripps and Vito Inglese;
to Richard Havers for holding everything together; to Kevin Gardner for his beautifully bright and clear design; to Elizabeth Stone for her editorial wisdom; to Rebecca Ellis for her impeccable proofreading.